PREFACE

A well-known motivational speaker often says, "Focus on the journey, not the destination. Joy is found not in finishing an activity but in doing it." In many areas of life this is an appropriate thought. From family road trips to educational processes to sports endeavors, the valuable lessons learned along the way can be life-altering— equipping us and preparing us for the next part of our own personal journey. Sometimes these parts of the journey are so wonderful that we don't want them to end—making the finish almost a letdown in the process.

However, while the "Focus on the journey, not the destination" quote may be true about many of life's activities, it is not equally true about life itself. In reality, while life is a journey, it is a journey that is going somewhere. Life on this planet is not some aimless meandering through time without purpose or direction. Our lives are journeys

PORTRAITS OF
ETERNITY

Exploring Life After Death

DISCOVERY HOUSE
PUBLISHERS®

Portraits of Eternity

© 2010 RBC Ministries

Discovery House Publishers is affiliated with
RBC Ministries, Grand Rapids, Michigan 49512

Cover Design: Stan Myers

Printed in the United States of America
10 11 12 / 10 9 8 7 6 5 4 3 2 1

CONTENTS

with a destination, and that destination is eternal in nature. Everyone—whether they believe it or not—will spend eternity somewhere.

Because the reality of our eternal destination is so vital to how we choose to live out our journey, we have compiled four of RBC's Discovery Series booklets that can provide for us some well-focused portraits of eternity. As we view these "portraits" of our destination, we can begin to answer questions like the following:

What happens after I die?

Am I accountable for how I have chosen to live in this life?

Are heaven and hell real?

What are they like?

These important questions deal with our future—and give us a look at the eternal life that is ahead for all of us. We trust that this glimpse at these *Portraits of Eternity* will assist you in making wise choices along your journey—choices that will help to prepare you for your eternal destination.

—*Bill Crowder*

Director of Ministry Content
Bible Teacher
RBC Ministries

One

IS THERE
LIFE AFTER DEATH?

Many people are fascinated with what have been called near-death experiences. Numerous books and TV programs have explored the stories of those who tell of life beyond death. Some people talk about a momentary release from the body as they lay on an operating table while doctors frantically tried to revive them. Others testify of serious accidents that momentarily seemed to break the grip of this life.

While these stories are inconclusive and arguable, we have convincing evidence that there is life after death—the record of what happened after the crucifixion of Jesus Christ. Long-time RBC Ministries research editor Herb Vander Lugt explores the record and the significance of these events as discussed by the apostle Paul in 1 Corinthians 15.

—*Martin R. De Haan II*

What Is The Easter Event?

The Bible tells us that one Friday almost 2,000 years ago, Jesus of Nazareth died on a cross and was buried before sunset. But it also records that He left the tomb on Sunday morning. That, according to Christians ever since, is the event of Easter. But not everyone would agree.

Rev. David Rankin, the former pastor of a large church in Grand Rapids, Michigan, has a different view of Easter. He told the religion editor of the *Grand Rapids Press* that he experienced the Easter event more than 30 years ago when he received a phone call informing him that his father had just died. He said that after the initial shock and feeling of overwhelming numbness, he gradually came to feel "an acceptance, with a purging and a healing, and a gradual drifting toward peace and understanding." To Rankin, this was "the Easter event." It enabled him to believe that in some way "death is conquered; that love builds enduring monuments; that every life has a purpose in the fullness of time."

These words may seem empty and meaningless to many people, and Rankin admits as much: "My heavens, if I really believed a person was resurrected from the dead, I'd go around shouting it all over the place, wouldn't I? I mean, that's amazing. I wouldn't just go to church and sing a few hymns."

Rankin thinks that belief in a literal resurrection is old-fashioned, unscientific, and unsuited for today's mindset. He insists that "dozens of cults" around the Middle East at the time Jesus lived were proclaiming heroes who were born of virgins, worked miracles, got themselves killed, and rose again. He therefore believes that the body of Jesus decayed like that of everyone else.

Rankin's talk about belief in a literal resurrection as old-fashioned and unscientific may upset believers who haven't studied the evidence. This view, however, that "dozens of cults" proclaimed a virgin-born, dying, and death-conquering redeemer has been shown false by British scholar and author C. S. Lewis and many others who are well-versed in the legends and myths of ancient times. But what Rankin said about getting excited if he believed in a literal resurrection really had an impact on me. I say that I believe it. And I really do. But I don't go around "shouting it all over the place." Like most of my Christian friends, I "go to church and sing a few hymns" instead of reflecting the excitement and joy this belief should produce.

Christians for almost 20 centuries have been declaring that the Easter event is the literal, bodily resurrection of Jesus Christ from the grave. They lived and died believing that they too would someday be brought back from death in a real body. This faith changed lives in the past. It still does today. This faith made heroes in the past. It still does today. Millions of believers throughout history have chosen to die as martyrs rather than deny their faith in the resurrection.

We believe that the Easter event is a real, historical occurrence with great significance for all of us today. Believing or not believing in it is a life-or-death matter. It determines our eternal destiny.

What Does Resurrection Mean?

When Christians talk about their future resurrection, they think of coming back from death in a real body—the same person they were when they died but just transformed.

Our future resurrection is not to be confused with the resuscitation of a corpse. It is more than that. This is what occurred with Lazarus (John 11) and in several other New Testament instances.

In these cases, the life process that had stopped somehow started going again in a manner somewhat similar to what occurs today when people are brought back from clinical death. The resuscitation of Lazarus by Jesus was a tremendous miracle because he had been dead four days. But later, he died again.

The Christian hope of resurrection is also far more than living forever in a ghostlike form. Cartoonists often depict the dead as floating about in space, their insubstantial form bearing some resemblance to their physical appearance on earth.

What we anticipate is living again in real bodies, knowing who we are, and recognizing one another.

Yet this new body, which Christians anticipate, will not be an exact replica of the one we have now. We believe, on the basis of what we read in the New Testament, that it will possess powers unknown today. We won't need telephones to communicate or vehicles to go from one place to another. The new body will be perfectly suited for life in a new, sinless environment—heaven.

To summarize, the God who originated life and invented biochemistry touched the cold, dead body of Jesus with His creative power. It was transformed into a perfect instrument for His immortal human spirit, passing through the grave clothes without unwrapping them and through the sealed tomb door without opening it (Matthew 28:1-2). One day, God will again use His creative power to give all of His children a body like the one Jesus received at His resurrection and in which He lives today.

I know this seems too wonderful to be true. I also confess that we who believe it aren't shouting from the housetops or displaying the joy we should. But the Bible tells us that this is precisely what every believer can anticipate. Moreover, it gives us solid reasons for believing what it says. One of the most comprehensive treatments of the subject of our future resurrection is found in 1 Corinthians 15. The remainder of this chapter will focus on this important passage.

Christ's Resurrection And Our Destiny

Jesus Christ came back from the grave in a real body, and so will all those who believe on Him. That's the essence of what the apostle Paul declared in 1 Corinthians 15. He dealt with the subject of resurrection with much detail because some church members in Corinth were saying that Christians should not expect a bodily resurrection after death. Although we don't know exactly what position they took regarding life after death, they probably taught that the soul or spirit of a believer lives on in heaven. We say this because it doesn't seem that people who believed that death ends everything would have been drawn to the Christian faith. It offered little by way of advantage in this world. In fact, the people who professed faith in Jesus Christ were the objects of scorn.

We can assume, then, that these professing Christians in Corinth believed in God, saw the death of Jesus Christ as paying the price for their sins, and professed faith in Him. But they must have carried into their new faith some wrong ideas from their pagan background. They had been taught that matter is evil and that at death we are released from the physical and taken into a purely spiritual form of existence—a definite improvement. They apparently tried to incorporate these pagan ideas into their Christian faith. This led them to teach that a future bodily resurrection is both impossible and undesirable.

Paul set out to correct this wrong thinking. He did so in six steps. First, he showed them that Jesus Christ did come back from death in a real body (vv. 1-11). Second, he explained how important it is to believe in the resurrection—that a denial of resurrection is a denial of the whole Christian message (vv.12-19,29-34). Third, he pointed out the vital connection between Christ's resurrection and the assurance of the Christian's resurrection (vv.20-28). Fourth, he emphasized the continuity and diversity of believers' resurrection bodies (vv.33-38). Fifth, he set forth some of the characteristics of our new bodies (vv.39-49). And finally, he concluded with a shout of triumph and a ringing challenge (vv.50-58).

■ A VERIFIABLE EVENT (*1 COR. 15:1-11*)

Moreover, brethren, I declare to you the gospel which I preached to you, which also you received and in which you stand, by which also you are saved, if you hold fast that word which I preached to you—unless you believed in vain. For I delivered to you first of all that which I also received: that Christ died for our sins according to the Scriptures, and that He was buried, and that He rose again the third day according to the Scriptures, and that He was seen by Cephas, then by the twelve. After that He was seen by over five hundred brethren at once, of whom the greater part remain to the present, but some have fallen asleep. After that He was seen by James, then by all the apostles. Then last of all He was seen by me also, as by one born out of due time. For I am the least of the apostles, who am not worthy to be called an apostle, because I persecuted the church of God. But by the grace of God I am what I am, and His grace toward me was not in vain; but I labored more abundantly than they all, yet not I, but the grace of God which was with me.

Therefore, whether it was I or they, so we preach and so you believed (vv. 1-11).

The first point Paul hammered home was this: "We know that Jesus came back from death in a resurrected body. Since this is a recent historical fact, no one has a right to say that a bodily resurrection is either impossible or undeniable." He reminded his readers of the message they had heard when they professed faith in Christ. It was the message that Jesus Christ died, paid the price for sin, was buried, and rose again just as the Old Testament Scriptures had prophesied. He also reminded them of some things they undoubtedly had heard before—how that Jesus, after His resurrection, had made many appearances to His followers. He didn't attempt to give a complete review of the appearances of Jesus as recorded in the Gospels. He singled out Christ's meeting with three individuals—Peter, James, and Paul himself. Then he mentioned two visits of Jesus to the apostles and one to a group of more than 500 people.

It's interesting to note that Paul regarded his Damascus-road experience as a valid personal encounter with the risen Christ, not as a mere vision. Faced with the apostles' personal testimonies, the heretics probably did not know what to say. They knew that Paul and the others were not liars. They could not produce evidence that the people who testified about their meetings with Jesus after His resurrection were mistaken. They had little choice but to acknowledge that Jesus

Christ was resurrected in a real body. This in turn confronted them with a defect in their reasoning. They had thought that resurrection from death was scientifically impossible and philosophically undesirable. By acknowledging that Jesus Christ rose from the grave, they were proving themselves wrong in their idea that a physical resurrection is an impossibility. Furthermore, by admitting that Jesus came back from death in a real body, they were refuting the idea that the body is inherently evil. God wouldn't have given Jesus Christ a new body if He viewed it as something evil.

The heretics had thought that resurrection from death was scientifically impossible and philosophically undesirable.

These people were living too close to the time of Christ's resurrection to effectively deny it. There were too many people around who could testify that they had seen the risen Christ. They simply could not explain away this great historical event any more than a person today can effectively deny the reality of the Holocaust.

There are people today who try to deny the Holocaust, but they don't get very far. Why? Mainly, because there are still many survivors of the Nazi concentration camps. In 1981, 6,000 of these survivors held a 4-day gathering in Jerusalem.

And though their numbers are dwindling, there are still survivors left who can recount the horrors. In an interview, Ernest W. Michel, a survivor of the Auschwitz and Buchenwald concentration camps and author of the Holocaust recollection book *Promises to Keep*, held up his hands and said, "These hands have carried off [for burial] more corpses than I care to remember. And some say that the Holocaust never happened! We know; we were there!"

The people to whom Paul wrote were living far closer to the time of Christ's resurrection than the people who met in Jerusalem in 1981 were to the Holocaust they survived. You and I, of course, are almost 2,000 years away from the resurrection. We can't talk to eyewitnesses like the people to whom Paul originally wrote his letter. How can we be assured that it really happened?

We can be certain because we have the written record of people who were there when it happened. The New Testament was written by first-century people—most of whom saw Jesus after His resurrection. This is something Christians always believed but for a long time could not prove.

In the 1800s and early 1900s, critics of the Bible claimed that the resurrection accounts came from the pens of men who lived during the second and third centuries. They spoke of these accounts as myths. But the critics can't honestly make that claim today. In recent years, manuscript copies of New Testament portions have been found that prove it was written when the contemporaries of Jesus Christ were still alive.

William Albright began his studies with the assumption that New Testament documents gradually developed over a period of several centuries. But he came to a different conclusion after studying the evidence. He declared, "There is no longer any solid basis for dating any book of the New Testament after AD 80" (*Recent Discoveries In Biblical Lands*, p.136).

Another scholar who changed his mind after careful research was John A. T. Robinson. For many years he assumed that the New Testament was written long after Christ's time. He decided he would do some investigation on his own. He was stunned by what he discovered. He came to the conclusion that the men he had respected had not been honest with the evidence. He decided that all the New Testament books, including the writings ascribed to the apostle John, were written before AD 54, an earlier date than most evangelical scholars had given. He had so much confidence in his conclusion that he wrote an article in *Time* magazine in which he challenged his colleagues to prove him wrong (March 21, 1977).

The evidence is in. The men who wrote the New Testament accounts of Christ's resurrection were around when it happened. We must believe what they wrote or think of them as gullible fools or deliberate liars. Gullible fools? Read the entire New Testament and draw your own conclusions. Deliberate liars? Not a chance! A conspiracy to deceive people breaks down when the people involved start getting into trouble.

Charles Colson, who was arrested and imprisoned for playing a role in the Watergate conspiracy during the presidential administration of Richard Nixon during the 1970s, said that as the scandal began to unravel, the conspirators, one by one, began to lay blame on each other. Loyalty went out the window! Each man was determined to protect his own hide. But with the apostles it was different. They faced something more serious than brief prison terms. One by one they were executed. But not one of them ever said, "We have been lying." Not one of them said, "We were deluded." Their behavior was that of sane men who knew and believed that what they were saying was true.

The resurrection of Jesus Christ is a verifiable historical event. You may ask, "If this is so, why do so many leading intellectuals disbelieve it?" One reason is moral. They do not want to believe, because this belief carries with it moral demands. They prefer to live by their own standards rather than submit to standards set by a holy God. The popular thing to do these days is to ignore the evidence, bypass all serious inquiry, and present imaginary accounts of Christ's life.

Hugh Schonfield and Gore Vidal have written books about Christ that are hailed as great by the secular media. They portray Jesus as a dishonest and immoral man, and they lightly dismiss the authentic accounts written by people who knew Him. This is willful unbelief.

A second reason many scholars refuse to give serious thought to the resurrection accounts stems from the human desire to be in step with the thinking of the time. Young people like to be with the "in" crowd. In secular colleges you get the best grades and the greatest applause if you go along with current thought. By and by, such people tend to abandon all ideas that a supernatural resurrection is even a possibility. Like an alcoholic who comes to the place where he sincerely thinks another drink will do him no harm, they drink at the fountain of secular thinking. They have no hope for eternity. They can find no abiding purpose or satisfaction in life. But they have so conditioned themselves that they will not even consider the possibility that Jesus Christ rose from death.

People do this to their eternal loss. The truth is that Jesus did come back from death. His resurrection is a verifiable event.

■ A CRUCIAL BELIEF (1 COR. 15:12-19,29-34)

Now if Christ is preached that He has been raised from the dead, how do some among you say that there is no resurrection of the dead? But if there is no resurrection of the dead, then Christ is not risen. And if Christ is not risen, then our preaching is empty and your faith is also empty. Yes, and we are found false witnesses of God, because we have testified of God that He raised up Christ, whom He did not raise up—if in fact the dead do not rise. For if the dead do not rise, then Christ is not risen. And if Christ is not risen, your faith is futile; you are still in your sins! (vv. 12-17).

There are two groups of people who refuse to believe in the resurrection of Christ and do so to their eternal harm: professed unbelievers and those who say they believe in Christ but reject the teaching that believers will be resurrected in real bodies. As noted earlier, some church members in Corinth were doing this. Some church leaders do so today. They say that the idea of a second coming of Christ and a bodily resurrection for all is outdated. But the apostle Paul made it clear that a person who does not believe in the resurrection of believers, no matter what the reason, is invalidating the entire gospel message.

We must take the same view of Christ's resurrection in the past as we do of our resurrection in the future. If Christ's resurrection was real, ours will be too. If future resurrection for believers is impossible or undesirable, the same must be said about the reported resurrection of Christ. And once the possibility or desirability of a bodily resurrection is denied, a process of reasoning is started that invalidates the gospel. Doubt is cast on either the intelligence or truthfulness of the apostles, and there is no reason for believing anything they wrote.

Paul wanted the Corinthians to see the serious nature of their error. They apparently thought they could deny a future bodily resurrection and still retain the basic elements of the Christian faith—forgiveness of sin, the power of the Holy

Spirit, and ultimate victory over sin and death. But Paul told them that this denial tore down the very foundation of New Testament salvation. Logic would demand that they reject the evidence of the apostles who told them that Christ had risen from the grave bodily. Their friends who had died in hope, perished. If the gospel only lasts until life ends, it is a bad bargain. "Then also those who have fallen asleep in Christ have perished. If in this life only we have hope in Christ, we are of all men the most pitiable" (vv.18-19).

After a brief digression (vv.20-28), Paul picked up this thread of thought again in verses 29-32:

> *What will they do who are baptized for the dead, if the dead do not rise at all? Why then are they baptized for the dead? And why do we stand in jeopardy every hour? I affirm, by the boasting in you which I have in Christ Jesus our Lord, I die daily. If, in the manner of men, I have fought with beasts at Ephesus, what advantage is it to me? If the dead do not rise, "Let us eat and drink, for tomorrow we die!"*

To emphatically make his point that denying a future bodily resurrection of believers is tantamount to rejecting the entire apostolic message, Paul declared that such a view makes becoming a Christian a foolish thing to do. He first referred to the fact that people were being "baptized for the dead."

This expression is difficult to understand. One

scholar said that he has found between 30 and 40 explanations. I will mention only three.

1. Some believe that a large-scale epidemic had brought on the death of many Christians who died before they could be baptized. Friends or relatives were being baptized for them.

2. Paul may have meant simply that new converts were being baptized regularly, filling the place in the church left by Christians who had died.

3. Another possibility is that Paul used the Greek preposition *huper*, which is translated "for," with the causal meaning "because of." In other words, people were being baptized (or saved) because of the testimony of Christians who had died.

No one knows for sure what Paul was referring to, but his point is clear: Baptism is foolish if we don't believe in the reality of our resurrection. Paul then said that he would be a fool to face the threat of death every day if he didn't have the hope of resurrection. If the gospel is not true and we have no real basis for hope, we might as well live by the philosophy, "Let us eat and drink, for tomorrow we die!" (v.32).

This suggests another reason resurrection belief is so crucial. Apparently, those Corinthians who abandoned the belief in resurrection abandoned other important teachings of the Bible as well. They began to go back to some of their old pagan ways and even became involved in immorality. They became bad companions. They gave evidence that they had never really come to know

vibrant as at the moment of resurrection.

Today the process of deterioration begins early. Professional athletes peak at about 30 years of age. Even with today's medical knowledge, only a few people live more than a century. Death comes.

The body, which has been deteriorating for years, swiftly decays—a few years in this body, but forever in our resurrection body.

The body we receive in resurrection will be marked by "glory," while "dishonor" is associated with the one we have now. The word translated "dishonor" in 1 Corinthians 15:43 is rendered "lowly" in Philippians 3:21. It is difficult to know exactly what Paul had in mind. William Barclay writes, "It may be that he meant that in this life it is through our bodily feelings and passions and instincts that dishonor can so easily come to life; but that in the life to come our bodies will no longer be servants of passion and of impulse, but the instruments of the pure service of God, than which there can be no greater honor."

Other commentators, like Godet and Hodge, view the term *dishonor* as referring to the humiliation people endure, when through old age or illness or accident they lose their faculties, become helpless, and need to be cared for like infants. In either case, the resurrection body will be far different. It will neither be an instrument of sin nor be subject to the humiliating physical impairments that so often precede death.

A third element in the perfection of the resurrection body is that it will be "raised in power." This is contrasted with our present weakness. We talk about people being strong, but this is a relative term. We are weak compared to many animals. Moreover, we can be killed by a fall, a drop of poison, a snake bite, a virus, and so on. We are so fragile. Our resurrection bodies will be powerful. It's difficult to imagine what we will be able to do. Since we will have bodies like Christ's resurrection body, it's likely that we will not need telephones to communicate or vehicles to transport us or computers to store information for us. Just thinking about going somewhere will get us there. Just desiring information will bring it to mind. Our bodies, including the brain, will be characterized by power.

■ A NEW DESIGN (VV. 44-49)

We now live in a body that is designed for earthly existence. The one we will receive in resurrection is designed for heaven.

It is sown a natural body, it is raised a spiritual body. There is a natural body, and there is a spiritual body. And so it is written, "The first man Adam became a living being." The last Adam became a life-giving spirit. However, the spiritual is not first, but the natural, and afterward the spiritual. The first man was of the earth, made of dust; the second Man is the Lord from heaven. As was the man of dust, so also are those who are made of dust; and as is the heavenly Man, so also are those who are heavenly. And as we have borne the image of the man of dust, we shall also bear the image of the heavenly Man (vv.44-49).

Paul distinguished between the earthly and the heavenly body by using the words *natural* and *spiritual* (v.44). On the surface, this may seem to teach that the resurrection body will have no substance, that it will be pure spirit. But that isn't the case. The Greek word translated "spiritual" is *pneumatikos*. Adjectives that end in *ikos* carry a functional or ethical meaning. The resurrection body will not be made up of spirit. That's not what Paul was saying. Rather, it will be enlivened by the redeemed human spirit. Our spirits will be in perfect tune with God and His will. Our body in heaven will respond perfectly to this redeemed spirit. In contrast, our present body is animated by and responds to earthly needs and desires. The rendering "natural" is right on target.

Paul developed the idea that our present bodies, being made of earth and designed for earth, are of a lower order than the one we will receive in heaven. We can probably assume that if Adam and Eve had not sinned, they would have reached the place where they would have been translated into their heavenly bodies. The body in which we now live is ours during our probationary period on earth. The choice that we make now determines whether we will remain forever on a lower level or rise to a higher life.

Our decision about Jesus Christ produces

results both in the present and the future. Paul declared, "As is the heavenly Man, so also are those who are heavenly" (v.48). Even though we are now subject to the temptations, pains, diseases, and deteriorating processes associated with our physical substance, we are already citizens of heaven (Phil. 3:20). In Ephesians 2:6, we are told that we have been made to "sit together in the heavenly places in Christ Jesus." A realization of what we now are in Christ certainly should make a great deal of difference in our lifestyle on earth.

Paul went on to depict our future state:

As we have borne the image of the man of dust, we shall also bear the image of the heavenly Man (v.49).

We will be perfectly designed for heaven because we will be just like our Savior.

■ A LIFE-CHANGING HOPE (1 COR. 15:50-58)

Paul's discussion of the resurrection now reaches a magnificent climax. His heart is full. His mind is running in high gear. You can feel the pulse of excitement in his words.

In verses 50-53, he began by summarizing what he had been saying.

Now this I say, brethren, that flesh and blood cannot inherit the kingdom of God; nor does corruption inherit incorruption. Behold, I tell you a mystery: We shall not all sleep, but we shall all be changed—in a moment, in the twinkling of an eye, at the last trumpet. For the trumpet will

sound, and the dead will be raised incorruptible,
and we shall be changed. For this corruptible must
put on incorruption, and this mortal must put on
immortality (vv. 50-53).

In our present body as flesh-and-blood beings, we cannot enter the eternal heavenly kingdom of God. We must be changed. We must receive a new body. And we will! God revealed to Paul the wonderful truth that a day is coming when the trumpet of heaven will sound, which will signal the return of Jesus Christ. "In the twinkling of an eye" believers who have died will receive their resurrection bodies and the living will be transformed from the earthly to the heavenly. All the redeemed will receive new, glorified bodies on that day! (See also 1 Th. 4:13-18.)

This thought caused Paul to burst forth in unbounded joy and exultation:

So when this corruptible has put on incorruption,
and this mortal has put on immortality, then shall be
brought to pass the saying that is written: "Death is
swallowed up in victory." "O Death, where is your
sting? O Hades, where is your victory?" The sting
of death is sin, and the strength of sin is the law. But
thanks be to God, who gives us the victory through
our Lord Jesus Christ (vv. 54-57).

The thought that the twin enemies of the human race—sin and death—will be totally conquered led the apostle to use graphic imagery. "Death is swallowed up in victory." Jesus Christ, through His death and resurrection, has so completely defeated death that, on that day in the future, death will be "swallowed up." It will be gone.

After this exultant expression of resurrection triumph, Paul taunted death. " 'O Death, where is your sting? O Death [Greek text], where is your victory?' The sting of death is sin, and the strength of sin is the law. But thanks be to God, who gives us the victory through our Lord Jesus Christ" (vv.55-57). The sting of death is sin because it is through sin that death came into the human race, and it is the awareness of sin that can make death a frightening experience. Moreover, it is by the law that sin gains strength—becomes rebellious. But in our place, Jesus Christ fulfilled the law by obeying it perfectly, and through His death He both paid the price for our sins and broke death's power. He won the victory over sin and death. And because He did, we will! We need have no fear in the face of death. Praise God!

Paul closed his climactic section with a practical appeal. He had been teaching. He had been praising God. From theology and praise he turned to exhortation in the form of a challenge:

Therefore, my beloved brethren, be steadfast, immovable, always abounding in the work of the Lord, knowing that your labor is not in vain in the Lord (v.58).

We have an indescribable glory to anticipate. In the light of this great expectation, we should persist in serving the Lord through thick and thin, gladly going beyond the call of duty. We can do this with the assurance that the reward will far outweigh the cost, no matter how deep the trials or how difficult the way.

Christ's Resurrection And You

If you have read this chapter, you know what Christians believe about Christ's resurrection and its meaning for them. You also know that the first followers of Jesus were so convinced of His resurrection that they spread the message with tremendous zeal and at great cost. Furthermore, you know that even though they died as martyrs one by one, every one of them remained steadfast.

Consider the fact that first-century Jewish believers started worshiping on the first day of the week instead of the seventh to commemorate Christ's resurrection. And don't ignore the testimony of such secular historians of ancient times as Tacitus, Josephus, Suetonius, and Pliny the Younger that the church was a powerful force in the Roman Empire by AD 64.

Reflect on the way simple people who believed were able to face torture and death for their faith. In AD 178 a Gallic slave girl, Blandina, was commanded to repudiate Christ or face torture and death. They murdered friends before her eyes. They heated her on a grid-iron. They threw her to wild beasts. They finally impaled her on a stake. She died praying for her tormentors. Her testimony led a 15-year-old boy, Ponticus, to follow her example.

The gospel still changes lives and gives courage. Thousands of believers died as martyrs during the twentieth century and even into the first part of this century. In fact, according to missions expert David Barrett, there were as many Christian martyrs in the twentieth century as in all nineteen previous centuries combined.

Think about these facts. Admit that you are a dying person among dying people. Admit your sinfulness and need of forgiveness.

Believe on Jesus Christ. You have all the evidence and understanding necessary. Once you believe, you will become a child of God (Jn. 1:12), and you will receive the Holy Spirit (1 Cor. 6:19). Your eyes will be opened. You will gain more understanding. Your life will be changed. And if you continue faithfully, you will become increasingly assured in your heart that you belong to Christ.

Two

What Does The Bible Say About Hell?

W hy did someone as good and loving as Christ spend so much time warning us about "the fire that shall never be quenched"—a place of "weeping and gnashing of teeth"? Why did He talk more about the fires of hell than about the joys of heaven?

Pursuing the subject of hell and thinking about a portrait of this horrible place are such sobering activities that many peope are more comfortable ignoring them. But there is no subject more deserving of our honest concern. In the following pages Herb Vander Lugt, who for many years was the senior research editor for RBC Ministries, leads us in a discussion that we hope will reawaken those of us who are living as if there is no tomorrow for the lost.

—*Martin R. De Haan II*

What Happened to the Subject of Hell?

Countless people among us seem obsessed with the subject of hell. Even irreligious individuals talk of "going to hell and back" for something they love. They speak of certainties as being "sure as hell," or impossibilities as occurring "when hell freezes over." And bad experiences are said to "hurt like hell." Many otherwise polite people regularly inject color, emotion, and profanity into their conversation by adding a casual or angry reference to hell to almost any combination of words.

Yet ironically, the more hell shows up in casual conversation, the less it is actually thought about—even in religious circles. The more such a word is used in an aggressive, profane way, the less threatening it seems to the user. Accordingly, the subject of hell has become as prevalent in street talk as it is absent in Sunday sermons.

It wasn't always that way. Historically, most religions have held openly to the idea of an after-death judgment followed by punishment for evildoers. In the *New Encyclopedia Britannica*, we read:

> *The view that hell is the final dwellingplace of the damned after a last judgment is held by the western prophetic religions: Zoroastrianism, Judaism, Christianity, and Islam. . . . Some modern theologians have again questioned the literalistic view but still*

hold that hell is, at least, a state of separation of the wicked from the good (Vol. 5, p. 814).

Our present reluctance to think seriously about the reality of future punishment may stem in part from an inadequate concept of God. We have forgotten that He is a God to be feared. The Russian theologian Berdyaev said, "It is remarkable how little people think about hell or trouble about it. This is the most striking evidence of human frivolity" (*The Destiny Of Man*, Scribner, 1937, p.33). What he wrote more than 70 years ago is even more true today than when he penned it.

We do not do people a favor when we remain silent about the subject of hell. Jesus, the prime example of God's love, spoke of hell repeatedly. He said that some would rise from death to "the resurrection of condemnation" (Jn. 5:29). He declared that those who go to hell enter the horrible place where "their worm does not die and the fire is not quenched" (Mk. 9:44,46,48). He also depicted it as a place of "outer darkness," where there "will be weeping and gnashing of teeth" (Mt. 8:12; 22:13; 25:30).

Bertrand Russell said he decided to become an atheist when he read the words of Jesus about hell. But did he act wisely? At least he was consistent. He realized that hell deserves to be taken seriously. He knew that it doesn't make sense to say you believe in Christ while rejecting what He and His book say about an eternal "lake of fire."

What Does the Bible Say About Hell?

■ HELL IS A PLACE OF CHOICE

People don't choose hell with a full understanding of what they are doing. They don't have a clear picture of the eternal happiness they will miss or the everlasting separation and darkness they will endure. But according to the Bible, hell is a place of choice.

As a result, the Bible repeatedly appeals to its readers to choose the way of life rather than the path of death and judgment. Over and over, Jesus Himself urged His listeners to make wise choices with questions like:

> *What will it profit a man if he gains the whole world, and loses his own soul? Or what will a man give in exchange for his soul?* (MK. 8:36-37).

Yet the same Bible also reminds us that most people will risk their eternal souls rather than feel obligated or indebted to the love and mercy of God. In some cases, this stubborn independence is easy to see. Some will even tell you that if there really is a heaven and a hell they would rather go to the place below because that's where their friends will be. Others say that heaven and God and eternal goodness sound boring. Still others are so angry at God for the pain and rejection that He has allowed them to experience that they have literally challenged

Him to send them to the devil and his place.

Most people, however, are merely ignoring the long-term possibilities of their own choices. They are either counting on the hope that God is too loving to send them to hell, or they are assuming that they aren't bad enough to be sent there. Many are so preoccupied with trying to survive day-to-day struggles that they have chosen not to worry about the future.

In the process, such people make personal choices for which they will be held accountable. Certainly they fail to understand the full weight of their choices. They fail to realize that just as the first man and woman made choices that resulted in enormous loss, so also we who are made in the image of God continue to be held accountable for the choices we make. With such choices and consequences in mind, the apostle Paul wrote:

> The wrath of God is revealed from heaven against all ungodliness and unrighteousness of men, who suppress the truth in unrighteousness, because what may be known of God is manifest in them, for God has shown it to them (ROM. 1:18-19).

As God's creatures, we owe Him glory and thanksgiving. God has a right to expect that we as a race and as individuals recognize His lordship, give Him thanks, and live in grateful obedience to Him. But in our pride, we have refused to glorify God as God. Instead, we have become preoccupied with ourselves and our own happiness. We have chosen to love ourselves rather than God—to glorify ourselves rather than the Lord. This is why "the wrath of God" (Rom. 1:18) rests upon the human race. This divine wrath is a terrible reality. It is God's revulsion against the things that contradict His holy being. It is God's reaction to those who choose evil while rejecting His love.

Some accuse God of vindictiveness. But we would be wise to withhold our criticism and respond as quickly as we can to God's invitation to escape the eternal fires. It was Christ Himself who urged us:

Enter by the narrow gate; for wide is the gate and broad is the way that leads to destruction, and there are many who go in by it. Because narrow is the gate and difficult is the way which leads to life, and there are few who find it (MT. 7:13-14).

Proportionately, this is still true. While religion is common all over the world, how many people do you know who actually and consistently love God and express their gratitude to Him? If you think carefully and honestly, you will have to admit that no one does. But Christians freely admit this and have placed their trust for salvation in Jesus Christ, believing that He paid for their sins when He died on the cross. When people refuse to believe on Him, they are choosing to stand on their own merits. To be placed on the road to heaven, we must acknowledge our sin, admit that we can't save ourselves, and place our trust in Jesus Christ. John 3:16 states:

For God so loved the world that He gave His only begotten Son, that whoever believes in Him should not perish but have everlasting life.

If you haven't chosen to believe on Jesus Christ, you are choosing the path to hell. Don't listen to the behaviorists who suggest that you have no real choices of your own.

Reject the postmodern thinking that says there is no established truth. Accept the teaching of the Bible. If you reject Christ, you will have no right to blame anyone but yourself when you someday find yourself in hell. You will have to admit that you made the wrong choice. You won't be able to blame God.

■ HELL IS A PLACE OF TRUTH

The second point we need to see is that hell is a place of truth. Even though it is sometimes described as a place of outer darkness, it is a place of the light of truth. Hell will finally expose the true nature of all who have consistently rejected the love and grace and mercy of God. In the meantime, the true nature of human hearts is often buried under deceptive appearances.

Now, most people don't think of themselves as deserving of everlasting punishment. Many who have chosen to live their lives apart from God don't look any different from others who openly admit their need of the forgiveness and mercy of Christ.

But present appearances are deceiving. While the Bible says that most people are headed for the lake of fire, many of them don't look as though they deserve a fire reserved for the devil and his angels. Evil men like Stalin or Hitler or serial killers might seem to qualify, but not the rank-and-file of people who seem to live basically decent lives.

Yet from the Bible's point of view, such evaluations are extremely misleading and even deceptive. The Bible shows us that the fires and blackness of hell will make eternal statements about (1) the true wickedness of public enemies and (2) the true wickedness of good people.

The Wickedness of Public Enemies.

In some respects, human wickedness is terrible to contemplate. Think of what God sees as He looks down on the world of mankind. He watches the murders, adulteries, thefts, fights, and physical and emotional torment that occur day and night in every part of the world. He sees the child abusers— their lust, cruelty, and heartlessness. He sees wives crying, children abandoned, friends and partners betrayed, governments oppressing, and religious leaders fleecing their trusting flocks.

It is the moral and spiritual condition that God has been patiently tolerating ever since man's fall into sin. Read the apostle Paul's timeless and universal description of the human condition:

They have all turned aside; they have together become unprofitable; there is none who does good, no, not one. Their throat is an open tomb; with their tongues they have practiced deceit; the poison

of asps is under their lips; whose mouth is full
of cursing and bitterness. Their feet are swift
to shed blood; destruction and misery are in
their ways; and the way of peace they have not
known. There is no fear of God before their eyes
(ROM. 3:12-18).

This is a striking picture of the dishonesty, the greed, the profanity, the deceitfulness, and the cruelty that continues to produce rapists, child molesters, embezzlers, and pornographers. When the judgment of God falls, and when such persons are sentenced to the lake of fire described in Revelation 20:11-15, the fire will make an eternal statement of truth about those who have lived their lives at the expense of others.

What we need to realize, however, is that Romans 3 was not written merely to tell the truth about those public enemies who will one day find their rightful place in hell. It also describes:

The Wickedness of Good People.

A closer look shows that Romans 3:10-18 doesn't just describe the judgment-deserving character of those we call public enemies. Verse 10 expresses the inclusive argument of the first three chapters of Romans, when it says of mankind, religious and non-religious alike:

There is none righteous, no, not one; there is
none who understands; there is none who seeks
after God. They have all turned aside; they have

together become unprofitable; there is none who
does good, no, not one (3:10-12).

We don't like to think that good people deserve
to go to hell. But our good impression of decent
law-abiding neighbors is not a real reflection
of the truth. We think naturally in very man-
centered ways rather than in the God-centered
measurement described in Romans 3. Man wasn't
made to be a decent public servant. He was made
to glorify his Maker and to enjoy Him forever. We
weren't made to live decent, self-serving lives. We
were made to depend gratefully on the love and
goodness of God. We weren't made just to abide
by the external requirements of civil and religious
law. We were made to worship God from our
hearts and to love one another as He has loved us.

When we measure ourselves by that evalua-
tion, the threat of hell becomes more of an issue.
The irresistible fire of judgment will expose the
enormous deception that now hides behind social
and religious courtesies and proprieties.

We have good reason to shudder at the
thought of standing in God's presence on our own
merits. If we're honest, we must admit that apart
from Christ we deserve to hear Him sentence us to
hell. In God's sight, no one is really a good person.

As many as have sinned without law will also perish
without law, and as many as have sinned in the
law will be judged by the law (for not the hearers
of the law are just in the sight of God, but the doers

*of the law will be justified; for when Gentiles, who
do not have the law, by nature do the things in the
law, these, although not having the law, are a law
to themselves, who show the work of the law written
in their hearts, their conscience also bearing witness,
and between themselves their thoughts accusing or
else excusing them) in the day when God will judge
the secrets of men by Jesus Christ, according to my
gospel* (ROM. 2:12-16).

All people, at one time or another, sense that
there is a God to whom they are morally accountable, that they have sinned, and that they need
divine forgiveness. But most men and women stifle
these disquieting thoughts. Some do so by denying
the existence of a personal God. Some do so by
saying that what we call sins are merely weaknesses.
Others affirm that God is so loving that He will
never punish anyone on the other side of death.
They don't want to acknowledge their sin and
believe on Jesus Christ. But the day is coming when
they will stand before God for final judgment.
There they will see themselves as they really are.
Stripped of all their self-righteousness, they will
recognize their guilt before God. And nothing less
than the lake of fire will ultimately tell the truth.

■ HELL IS A PLACE OF FAIR TREATMENT

We have seen that hell is the place people choose,
even if unknowingly, when they go their own way
instead of listening to God. We have also noted
that hell is a place that will forever tell the truth

about the real character of those who have rejected and resisted God's provision for their salvation.

We are now ready to consider a third fact—that hell will be a place of fair treatment. Before anyone goes there, that person will stand at a final judgment to determine the exact degree of punishment he or she will receive. God will be perfectly fair.

The final judgment is depicted graphically in Revelation 20:11-15. This is the great white throne judgment. The Judge is none other than Jesus Christ (Jn. 5:24-30). All the unsaved will receive new bodies and will stand to be judged. Then the books containing the life record of every person and the one special Book of Life will be opened. The opening of these books shows that those who rejected God's gift of salvation will receive perfect justice.

In Romans 2:1-16, Paul pointed out that God will look at what people have done with their privileges and opportunities, and that He will be completely impartial and fair (vv.5-11). Those who possessed His Word, the law of verses 12-14, will be held accountable for their response to it. Those who never received special revelation will be held accountable only for what they knew (vv.14-16).

Jesus taught this same principle when He said that the servant who knew his master's will and disobeyed would be beaten with "many stripes," but that the servant who had less knowledge would be beaten with "few" (Lk. 12:47-48).

No judge or jury fully understands the person on trial. No human being can evaluate the exact degree of accountability in himself or anyone else. We are all profoundly influenced by hereditary and environmental factors beyond our control. Yet we make choices after weighing options. Therefore, we are all accountable—at least to some degree. And God understands to what extent. He also knows how much we need His mercy.

When the young man who died in a gang war stands before Jesus Christ, he will find that the Lord understands all the circumstances of his short, violent, and troubled life—his absent father, his immoral mother, his disadvantaged peers, his complete ignorance of the gospel message, and his despair. The Lord Jesus will take all these factors into consideration. He knows exactly the degree of responsibility of this young man and will give him a sentence that perfectly suits his offense.

The rich, respectable landlord who died without Christ may receive a far more severe sentence than most of his tenants, even those who had many brushes with the law. The Lord Jesus will take into account their respective privileges. He will see perfectly the underlying greed, selfishness, and pride of this man. He will understand the sense of despair that was a factor in some of the wrongs done by the tenants. All will receive fair treatment. God, the holy moral Governor of the universe, will dispense perfect justice to all wrongdoers.

The awesome picture of final judgment in Revelation 20:11-15 led Thomas Carlyle to exclaim: "What a magnificent conception is that of a final

judgment! A righting of all the wrongs of the ages."
The Lord Jesus Christ will take into account every
circumstance, overlooking nothing. He will be the
Supreme Court of the universe. No one will be able
to appeal His decisions. In fact, no one will feel the
need to do so. Every person will acknowledge Him
as Lord and admit that His verdict has been absolutely fair and right. It is at this time that everyone
will recognize Him to be all He claimed to be, fulfilling the words of Philippians 2:9-11.

> *Therefore God also has highly exalted Him and
> given Him the name which is above every name,
> that at the name of Jesus every knee should bow,
> of those in heaven, and of those on earth, and of
> those under the earth, and that every tongue should
> confess that Jesus Christ is Lord, to the glory of
> God the Father.*

■ HELL IS A PLACE OF LOST HOPE

We have seen that people choose hell by rejecting
the light they have received from God. We have
seen that everyone is a sinner whose selfishness and
pride call for divine punishment—even the nice
non-Christian who has so many fine qualities. We
have seen that Jesus Christ is going to judge every
person individually and will sentence him/her to
receive exactly what he/she deserves. Now we are
ready to develop the solemn fact that hell is a place
of lost hope. We must take the love-filled, tear-
marked Jesus seriously when He warned:

Do not fear those who kill the body but cannot kill the soul. But rather fear Him who is able to destroy both soul and body in hell (Mt. 10:28).

We will consider the final and irreversible nature of this loss in three steps: First, we will examine the so-called "universalist" or "second chance" passages in the Bible. Second, we will consider the passages that speak of hell as a place of "destruction." Third, we will study the implications of the fact that the terms *everlasting* or *eternal* often appear in reference to hell.

The "Second Chance" Passages.

We who believe on Jesus Christ and therefore are confident that we will go to heaven would like to see everyone get there eventually. We would very much like to find evidence in the Bible that the lost will get another chance to be saved after death. And there always have been teachers who have held the viewpoint of another opportunity after death. Some Bible students refer to themselves as universalists because they believe that eventually everyone or almost everyone will end up in heaven. They believe that 1 Peter 3:18-20 and 4:6, and 1 Timothy 2:5-6 imply the hope of another chance after death. They view Acts 3:21, 1 Corinthians 15:22, Philippians 2:9-11, and Colossians 1:20 as verses which imply that almost all will eventually be among the redeemed. Let's take a look at these passages.

First Peter 3:18-20. These verses declare that "Jesus preached to the spirits in prison," specifically to contemporaries of Noah. Some Bible interpreters believe that Peter was referring to the preaching done by Noah while he was building the ark. Others teach that between His death and resurrection Jesus went to the realm of the unsaved dead and announced what He had done. Still others believe He went to the prison house for fallen angels and announced His redeeming work to them. We may choose any of these interpretations. It is a difficult passage, to be sure. Just as certain, however, is that we should not take a difficult passage like this and use it to overrule other passages like Hebrews 9:27, which states, ". . . it is appointed for men to die once, but after this the judgment."

First Peter 4:6. This is another verse often used to prove that people will receive another chance. Peter wrote:

> For this reason the gospel was preached to those who are dead, that they might be judged according to men in the flesh, but live according to God in the spirit.

This verse refers to the proclamation of the gospel to living people who later died. The preaching was done while these individuals were alive. They were judged harshly by the world, but they now enjoy the bliss of heaven. They are far better off than those who gained the praise of the world but must face God's judgment after death.

First Timothy 2:5-6. This passage is also quoted as a proof of a second chance after death. It tells us:

> There is one God and one Mediator between God

and men, the Man Christ Jesus, who gave Himself
a ransom for all, to be testified in due time.

Those who view this passage as offering another
chance for salvation after death point out that the
ransom price was paid for all, and that it will be
"testified" to all "in due time." Some people in this
world never receive an opportunity to hear the gospel, and many who do, hear it under very unfavor-
able circumstances. Therefore, "in due time," under
conditions more favorable after death, the gospel of
salvation will be offered to all. The context, however, eliminates such an interpretation. Paul made
this statement in connection with his injunction that
God's people pray for all men (not just for a small
select company), and with his declaration that God
desires all people to be saved (not just Israelites). He
asserted that Christ's ransom was universal in avail-
ability and that the gospel testimony is to go out
everywhere. There is no indication here of another
gospel offer after death.

Acts 3:21. Peter spoke of "the times of restoration of all things," and this to some Bible scholars
implies the idea that in the end all will be saved. But
a careful study of this verse makes it clear that Peter
was speaking about the restoration of Israel as predicted by the Old Testament prophets. They spoke
of Israel's return to the land and the restoration of
the theocracy under David's Son, but they never
predicted a day when the unsaved dead would be
converted and translated to heaven.

First Corinthians 15:22. Paul's words "For as

in Adam all die, even so in Christ all shall be made alive" are sometimes taken to mean that all will eventually be saved. But that isn't what Paul said.

He declared the simple truth that just as every person dies because he is united with Adam as a member of the sinful human race by natural birth, so every person who is united with Christ shall experience a glorious resurrection. We did nothing to become a member of the human race, but we must believe on Christ and be born again to enter Christ's family. We who have done this are now "in Christ" and therefore recipients of eternal life.

Colossians 1:20. Paul declared that God's purpose is "to reconcile all things to Himself . . . through the blood of His cross." Standing by itself, this seems to teach that eventually every creature will be brought into a saving relationship with God. William Hendriksen quotes a minister who used this verse as the basis for the following statement: "In the end everybody is going to be saved. I have hope even for the devil."

> *As much as we would like to think that ultimately all will be saved, we cannot honestly use the Scriptures to build a case for it.*

But when we interpret this verse in the light of the many passages that clearly distinguish between a resurrection to condemnation and a resurrection to blessedness, we see Colossians 1:20 as teaching that through the blood of the cross God provided for the restoration of the whole universe to the harmony He intended for it—the harmony that was broken through sin. The day is coming when all creatures will be brought into subjection to God. They will acknowledge the authority of the triune God and submit to Him. They will confess the lordship of Christ to the glory of the Father (Phil. 2:10-11). In the case of the evil spirits and unredeemed human beings, this subjection will be imposed, not welcomed. On the other hand, the good angels and redeemed people will submit joyfully and rejoice in the fact that rebellion has ceased and a new harmony exists in God's universe.

No, as much as we would like to think that ultimately all will be saved, we cannot honestly use the Scriptures to build a case for it.

The "Destruction" Passages.

Having pointed out the solemn fact that the Bible does not give us reason to look for a second chance for salvation after death, we are now ready to consider the implications of the word *destruction* when used to describe the destiny of the wicked and unbelieving. In 2 Thessalonians 1:9, for example, we are told that those who refuse to know God and to obey the gospel "shall be punished with everlasting destruction from the presence of the Lord." The word here is *olethros*, the same word used in 1 Corinthians 5:5, 1 Thessalonians 5:3, and 1 Timothy 6:9.

Jesus made the solemn declaration, "And do

not fear those who kill the body but cannot
kill the soul. But rather fear Him who is able to
destroy both soul and body in hell" (Mt. 10:28).
The Greek word here for "destroy" is *apollumi*. It
occurs scores of times in the New Testament.
Jesus used this term when He said that new wine
would "ruin" an old wineskin (Lk. 5:37) and when
He referred to the food we eat as "the food which
perishes" (Jn. 6:27).

The fact that the Greek terms sometimes rendered "destroy" or "perish" can mean "to bring to
an end" or "cease to exist" has led some Bible students to say that the unsaved will be resurrected,
judged, punished according to their works, and
then annihilated. They point out that the doctrine
of human immortality comes from Greek thought
rather than the Hebrew or Greek Scriptures. Paul
declared that God "alone has immortality, dwelling in unapproachable light, whom no man has
seen or can see" (1 Tim. 6:16). These Bible scholars are well aware of our Lord's statement that the
unredeemed go into "everlasting punishment" (Mt.
25:46). But they see eternal extinction as eternal
punishment, pointing out that Jesus didn't say
eternal conscious punishment.

These teachers, however, are not simple anni-
hilationists. They take seriously the Bible verses
that speak of the resurrection, judgment, and
appropriate punishment of the lost. But they
believe that the eventual destiny of the unsaved
will be extinction. They view hell as a grim real-

ity. They recognize that the terms *destroy* and *destruction* can mean more than "annihilation." They declare that "the fire will not be quenched" until God has vindicated His holiness in the punishment of all sin. However, they look forward to a point in eternity after which nothing sinful or painful will exist in the entire universe.

Most orthodox Bible scholars have not accepted this teaching. They have difficulty equating "eternal punishment" with "eternal nonexistence." They also think of mankind in God's image as created for an eternal conscious destiny in either heaven or hell.

The "Forever and Ever" Passages.

We have shown that the Bible does not promise or even imply that the lost will have another chance for salvation after death. We have also observed that the Greek words translated "perish" or "destroy" in relation to hell can either denote eternal conscious ruin or eventual extinction of being. So it's important for us to consider the Greek terms that are usually translated "everlasting," "eternal," or "forever and ever" in the Bible. In relation to hell, do they really denote endlessness? And do they indicate that the lost will endure conscious punishment throughout all eternity?

In view is the Greek word *aion* (usually rendered "forever" or "eternal") and the Greek expression *tous aionas ton aionon* (normally rendered "forever and ever"). In and by themselves, they do not necessarily denote eternity. When Jewish scholars translated the Old Testament from Hebrew to Greek, they used the term *aion* to denote the "everlasting hills" of Genesis 49:26 and to depict the servant who voluntarily had his ear pierced to indicate that he wished to remain with his master "forever" (Dt. 15:17). Paul counseled Philemon to receive Onesimus back as his slave "forever" (Phile. 15). In all of these cases, the word *aion* relates to this world only, not to eternity. But the same term was also used to depict God as the eternal One, "from everlasting to everlasting" (Ps. 41:13; 90:2; 106:48). It is obvious that the context must determine when this term denotes a span of time and when it denotes absolute endlessness.

Kittel's *Theological Dictionary Of The New Testament* tells us that when *aion* is used in any of its forms in relation to this world, it denotes the "time or duration of the world." But when used of God or the world entered at death, it denotes "timeless eternity." The Greek mind basically thought in terms of two ages—the present age that will end and the future age that is timeless. The New Testament writers "borrowed" this usage. Whenever they used the word *aion* in relation to God, spiritual realities, or life after death, they had absolute timelessness or never-ending eternity in mind (see Vol.1, pp.197-209).

The words *aion* and *aionion* are used several times in relation to the fate of those who die in unbelief or rebellion. Jesus declared that after His judgment of the nations the lost will "go away into everlasting punishment, but the righteous into eternal life" (Mt. 25:46). Of the people who will worship the Antichrist and his image, we read, "And the smoke of their torment ascends forever and ever; and they have no rest day or night" (Rev. 14:11). In addition, the beast, the false prophet, and Satan will

> *The future of those who die as unbelievers or rebels is not pleasant to contemplate.*

be cast into the lake of fire, where "they will be tormented day and night forever and ever" (Rev. 20:10).

The Greek word translated "tormented" in these last two verses is *basanizo* which, according to the lexicons, denotes "physical or mental distress, torture, or harassment." Only conscious beings can suffer this way. Therefore, we must conclude that eternal *conscious* suffering is denoted in these passages.

In summary, the future of those who die as unbelievers or rebels is not pleasant to contemplate. When Jesus talked about hell, He spoke of "weeping and gnashing of teeth" (Mt. 8:12), of "the fire that shall never be quenched" (Mk. 9:43,45), and of a place "where their worm does not die" (Mk. 9:44,46,48). Even if many verses are inconclusive regarding the eternal conscious suffering of the lost, Revelation 14:11 and 20:10 indicate that at the very least, some of the lost will suffer conscious torment for all eternity.

We must be careful that we do not go beyond the Scriptures and portray hell as a place where all the lost will scream in pain forever and ever. This picture gives a wrong impression of God. He is not only perfectly holy and just, but He will be absolutely fair in punishment. Jesus pointed out that on the day of judgment the inhabitants of ancient Sodom would be treated with more mercy than the people in Judea who had deliberately rejected Him and His apostles (Mt. 10:15). He also spoke of the servant who would be punished lightly because he had little knowledge of God's will (Lk. 12:48).

C. S. Lewis, in his book *The Great Divorce*, pictures the lost as having to live with themselves and one another unchanged from what they were on earth. He portrays them as moving slowly and inexorably farther and farther from reality through eternity. He admitted that his work was not a theological treatise and didn't want it to be interpreted as such. But he wanted to make us realize that even if there were no extreme physical pain, hell would be a terrible place. It is a fact that actions form habits and habits develop character. Unless a person has been born again through faith in Christ, he will go into eternity with a nature that has been fixed in this life. He dies a sinner and will be a sinner forever, but he will be unable to carry out his evil thoughts or inclinations. He will be in torment, but his nature will be so twisted by his evil desires that he will prefer the misery of hell to the kind of activities that occupy the saints in heaven.

It is perhaps wise for us to avoid excessive speculation about the suffering of hell. We can't understand the concept of eternity. And we don't know just what the bodies of the unredeemed in hell will be like. The biblical doctrine of hell is designed to warn sinners. It is designed to motivate believers to do all they can to reach people with the gospel. It is designed to show us how terrible sin is in the sight of an awesomely holy God. Therefore, although we cannot visualize either the timelessness of eternity or the exact nature of hell's suffering, we can be moved to godly fear and proper action. And we can ultimately trust God to do what is right by friends and relatives who for one reason or another refuse the gospel. With Abraham of old we can ask the rhetorical question, "Shall not the Judge of all the earth do right?" (Gen. 18:25), and leave the matter to Him.

What's The Fate Of Those Who Never Heard?

Many people have gone through this life without even once hearing about Jesus Christ. Even among those who live in cultures where Christian holidays like Christmas and Easter are observed, there are multitudes who never really hear the gospel. And some who have had contact with professing Christians never give Jesus Christ serious consideration because of what they see in the lives of people who claim to be His followers.

What about such people who will die without ever having heard a clear presentation of the gospel? Can we assume that God will find some way to open the doors of heaven to them? We would like to believe that. But the Scriptures make it clear that those who haven't heard the gospel are lost just as surely as those who refuse to believe on Christ. Jesus declared that He Himself is the only way to God (Jn. 14:6). Peter boldly told the Jewish rulers who had arrested him, "Nor is there salvation in any other, for there is no other name under heaven given among men by which we must be saved" (Acts 4:12). Paul referred to all who don't know Jesus as "those who are perishing" (2 Cor. 4:3) and described the Gentile world before the time of Christ as "having no hope and without God in the world" (Eph. 2:12). The heartbreaking fact is that people who have never heard the gospel are on their way to a Christless eternity.

> We can trust God to do right by all those who die without having heard the saving gospel of Jesus Christ.

God will hold those who never heard the gospel responsible for what they did with the light that they had in this world. Paul said of the pagans that God had revealed Himself to them in nature (Rom. 1:18-21) and in conscience (Rom. 2:12-16). They must give an account of what they did with this light and will be punished accordingly.

Sir Norman Anderson, a respected evangelical, has pointed out that some who never hear the gospel become conscious of their sinfulness, abandon all efforts to earn God's favor, and cry out for forgiveness. He contends that they are to be viewed in the same situation as most of the Old Testament believers who were saved by God's grace through faith even though they had only a vague concept of Christ. He writes, "The believing Jew was accepted and blessed not because of the prescribed animal sacrifices he offered, nor even his repentance and abandonment to God's mercy, but because of what God Himself was going to do in His only Son at the cross of Calvary" (*Christianity And World Religions: The Challenge Of Pluralism*, p.153).

It's not imperative that we accept Anderson's suggestion, because the Bible doesn't tell us about the fate of these "noble" pagans. But we can be certain about one thing: We can trust God to do right by all those who die without having heard the saving gospel of Jesus Christ. And that is all we need to know!

The Fire Of Hell

The term *fire* is often used in connection with the punishment of the lost. In Revelation 20, the expression "lake of fire" occurs three times to denote the final destiny of God's enemies.

Fire is also associated with hell because of the Greek word *gehenna*, the term most often employed to denote the place where the lost will go after death and judgment. It occurs 11 times in the gospels and once in the rest of the New Testament (Jas. 3:6). The word itself referred to "the valley of Hinnom," just south of Jerusalem. It was there that the Israelites under Ahaz and Manasseh (2 Chr. 28:3; 33:6) placed children on a fiery altar dedicated to the god Molech. The specific place where this was done was called Tophet (literally "fire place"). There is a strong tradition that the valley became a city dump where refuse and the bodies of criminals were burned. The terrible reputation of this valley plus its association with fire and judgment made it an apt symbol for the place of final punishment for the wicked.

So should we portray hell as a literal furnace of fire where all the lost will scream in pain throughout all eternity? The Church Fathers, Luther, Calvin, all the classical theologians, and present-day evangelical leaders like Francis Schaeffer and J. I. Packer say an emphatic no.

They point out that God will lightly punish those who did not know much about His expectations (Lk. 12:48). A hell in which all burn in a literal fire does not allow for significant degrees of punishment.

Then too, it's important to remember that the Bible often uses fire as a symbol. In 1 Corinthians 3:12-15, our works (or doctrines) are portrayed as "wood, hay, straw" that will be consumed by the fire of judgment or as "gold, silver, precious stones" that will endure the fire.

In James 3:5-6 the tongue is a "fire," causes "fire," and is itself "set on fire by hell." Hebrews 12:29 declares that "our God is a consuming fire." Jude 23 speaks of people who have been doctrinally misled and are in need of being snatched "out of the fire."

In all of these references, the fire is symbolic.

The Bible presents a literal hell as the place of eternal punishment for all who die in unbelief or rebellion. Unscriptural and repulsive overstatements about hell have turned some people away from the gospel. Such excesses have also caused some true believers to ignore the biblical teaching about hell or to develop false doctrines like universalism. But a sensitive and accurate treatment of this truth can be used by God to strengthen Christians and to awaken sinners to their need of Christ.

Trust God To Do Right

The woman was convinced that she was a sinner who needed God's forgiveness. She also believed the good news that Jesus died on the cross for her sins and destroyed the power of death through His resurrection. But she balked when I suggested that she receive Jesus as her Savior. She said she wasn't sure she wanted to go to heaven if her parents were in hell. They had been churchgoing, loving, honest people. But she didn't think they had ever heard the gospel clearly presented.

Sensing her resistance, I said, "Neither you nor I know for sure where your parents will spend eternity. It's possible that they believed Jesus died for their sins and trusted Him to save them. But we can be sure of one thing—God will do right by them. Trust Him and do what He says. Receive Jesus as your Savior." She did, and today she is a strong Christian woman.

We don't like the idea of eternal punishment. We may even find ourselves repulsed by the concept. But we need to be careful. God sees and understands infinitely more than we do.

He has proven His love in so many ways, especially providing salvation through Jesus Christ (Jn. 3:16; Rom. 5:8). He wants you to place your trust in His Son. Listen to Him, accept His salvation, and trust Him to do what is right to you and to all mankind. Accept His warning to escape "the fire that shall never be quenched—where 'their worm does not die, and the fire is not quenched'" (Mk. 9:44,46,48).

Defining Our Terms

Annihilationism—the idea that people will not suffer eternal conscious torment in hell but will eventually be consumed or obliterated in judgment, ceasing to exist.

Beast—the violent and aggressive endtime person, also known as the Antichrist, who will deceive the nations before being sentenced by God to everlasting torment.

Damned, condemned—the terrible state of those sentenced to eternal separation from God.

Destruction—to be ruined or consumed. The word is used repeatedly in the Bible to describe God's plan to bring His enemies first to the grave and then ultimately to the fires and darkness of hell.

Devil/Satan—the powerful personal spirit being who through pride and hatred has become the chief adversary of God and will lead countless fallen angels and humans to rebellion and a destiny of eternal punishment.

Evangelicals—a label describing those who accept the good news that Jesus is the Christ, the only Son of God, who lived a perfect life, died for our sins, was buried, and rose again on the third day to offer eternal life to all who would believe in Him.

Evil—the absence or opposite of good, love, and godliness; a condition of spiritual independence that resists God's plan for us.

False Prophet—the endtime person who will use supernatural power to bring honor to the Antichrist before joining him in a place of everlasting torment.

Fear Of God—a healthy dread of resisting or rebelling against God, with the result of moving toward God rather than away from Him. Properly understood, it is reverential awe that results in trust and love for God.

Gospel—the good news that Christ died for our sins, that He was buried, and that He rose from the grave to save all who will trust Him.

Hell—the place of final judgment created for the devil, his angels, and all who die without making peace with God. Described as the lake of fire and a place of outer darkness where the torment is characterized by weeping and gnashing of teeth.

New Age—a world-view that sees man as being

one with the spiritual life-force of the universe, capable of shaping his own destiny through the development of mind and potential.

Soul—the immaterial part of man that includes the intellect, emotion, and will. It exists with or without the body.

Pagan, Sinner, Wicked, Lost—terms describing those who, for lack of faith in Christ, are outside the circle of His forgiveness and life.

Salvation—the rescue God offers us. It may refer to deliverance from temporary physical harm, but in the highest sense it speaks of God's loving offer to save us from the past, present, and future effects of sin. It is available only in the name of Christ, who gave His life to save all who trust Him to deliver them from eternal separation from God.

Self-righteous—a term that describes one who thinks he is good enough to merit heaven by personal effort rather than by believing that goodness is a gift of God received through faith in Christ.

Universalist—one who believes that everyone will eventually be saved and brought into a right relationship with God.

Wrath Of God—the perfect and patient anger of God that will consume all who persistently and finally refuse to acknowledge His rightful place in their lives.

Three

JUST BEFORE HEAVEN:
The Judgment Seat
Of Christ

Contained in the pages of this chapter is a truth that brought one of the wisest men who ever lived out of late-life disillusionment. Overcome by a sense of life's repetitious boredom and profoundly disturbed by the temporary, pointless nature of existence, Israel's King Solomon finally came to a renewing truth—one that is presented here by well-known author J. Oswald Sanders in this excerpt from his book *Heaven: Better By Far*.

What makes the Christian life significant and what gives even repetitious thoughts and boring work lasting value is the awareness that at some time in the future our loving and merciful God will weigh the value of everything we have done (Eccl. 12:14).

J. Oswald Sanders is now with his Lord. It is our privilege to provide you with his words that paint a portrait of the events that will happen "Just Before Heaven."

—*Martin R. De Haan II*

The Second Coming and The Judgment Seat Of Christ

In his book *What About Heaven?* W. Graham Scroggie wrote, "The revelation of a judgment seat for believers is a further evidence that the fullness of heaven is not entered upon and enjoyed by any until after the advent and the resurrection. Christians who throughout these nineteen hundred years have passed on have not yet been judged as to their faithfulness or unfaithfulness. That does not take place when we die, but will do so on the eve of the consummation of redemption, of that state which will be perfect, serviceable, and eternal" (p.108).

What will the second coming and the judgment seat of Christ mean to us?

The promised second coming of our Lord will mean for us the beginning of the promised joys of heaven. It will mean being with Christ, which is better by far. But that will not be the whole story. It will precipitate the greatest series of judgmental events in the history of the world. Paul foretold a resurrection of the righteous and of the wicked, when all will face the outcome of deeds done in the body (Acts 24:15).

The prospect of a coming day of judgment is one of the least popular articles of the Christian faith and is denied even by some who claim to be Christians. But it is not a concept that is peculiar to Christianity; it is common to other religions and philosophies as well. The Buddhist, for example, believes in 16 hells. The universal conscience of humanity bears witness to a sense of guilt, a feeling of moral responsibility to a supreme being or god. People are accountable to God, and He will reward good and punish evil.

The distinctive tenet of Christianity is that God has delegated this office to His Son, Jesus Christ, who will judge the living and the dead. "For the Father judges no one, but has committed all judgment to the Son" (Jn. 5:22). "He [Jesus of Nazareth] commanded us to preach to the people, and to testify that it is He who was ordained by God to be Judge of the living and the dead" (Acts 10:42).

No one who accepts the authority of Christ and the authenticity of His Word can doubt that there is a judgment to come. But there is a vast difference between the judgment of believers and that of nonbelievers. For the believer, there lies ahead the bema or judgment seat of Christ (2 Cor. 5:10). For the impenitent, there is the inescapable prospect of standing before the great white throne of judgment (Rev. 20:5,11-12).

It is neither possible nor necessary to compile an exact timetable for these awesome events; it is the absolute certainty of them that is important. Hebrews 9:27 says that "it is appointed for men to die once, but after this the judgment." We must bear in mind that when these events do take place, the measures of time and space as we now know them will have no relevance.

But, speaking in terms with which we are familiar, would it not be reasonable to conclude that, since the "day of salvation" has extended over two millennia, we need not try to compress the day of judgment into a brief period? Conversely, does this judgment necessarily require a long time as we know it? In these days of the marvels of the Internet and the immeasurably greater marvel of the human brain, coupled with the omniscience of God, the slowness of our judicial processes affords no comparison. It is a well-established phenomenon that, in crisis, the whole content of a life may be flashed before the mind of a person in a moment of time.

In this chapter, we are concerned only with the judgment of believers at the bema. This is one of the most important events connected with the return of Christ, as far as the believer is concerned. "For we must all appear before the judgment seat of Christ, that each one may receive the things done in the body, according to what he has done, whether good or bad" (2 Cor. 5:10).

Does this mean that we will have to wait until that day to know whether we are saved or lost? Does Scripture not teach that upon believing in Christ we pass from death to life and will not come into condemnation?

Indeed it does. The explanation of 2 Corinthians 5:10 lies in the fact that Scripture recognizes two kinds of judgment. There is the judgment in criminal proceedings where the judge sits on the bench, hears the evidence, and decides the guilt, condemnation, or acquittal of the person charged. Then there is the judgment of the umpire, or referee who, as at the Olympic games, ascends his judgment seat to pronounce the winner and award the prize, because the victor has run fairly and well. Of course, the corollary is that those who have not run fairly and well "suffer loss" and win no prize. It is this second judgment seat that Paul has in view in this verse.

A person's eternal destiny is already determined in this life, according to whether or not he or she has trusted Christ for salvation. "So then each of us shall give account of himself to God" (Rom. 14:12). Few verses of Scripture are more soul-searching than this. Daniel Webster, the noted American statesman, on being asked what was the greatest thought he had ever entertained, replied, "The greatest thought that has ever entered my mind is that one day I will have to stand before a holy God and give an account of my life."

The judgment seat of Christ, then, is His "umpire" seat. The primary purpose of His judgment is to assess and reward believers for the manner in which we have used our opportunities and discharged our responsibilities. The basis on which we will be judged is stated in clear terms: "that each one may receive what is due him for the things done while in the body, whether good or bad" (2 Cor. 5:10 NIV).

But motives as well as deeds will be taken into account. "Therefore judge nothing before the time, until the Lord comes, who will both bring to light the hidden things of darkness and reveal the counsels of the hearts" (1 Cor. 4:5).

In a very penetrating paragraph Paul told us how this process is carried out:

> *For no other foundation can anyone lay than that which is laid, which is Jesus Christ. Now if anyone builds on this foundation with gold, silver, precious stones, wood, hay, straw, each one's work will become clear; for the Day will declare it, because it will be revealed by fire; and the fire will test each one's work, of what sort it is. If anyone's work which he has built on it endures, he will receive a reward. If anyone's work is burned, he will suffer loss; but he himself will be saved, yet as through fire (1 COR. 3:11-15).*

Whatever else this paragraph teaches, it makes clear that there can be a saved soul but a lost life because of unfaithfulness in the stewardship of life.

What do gold, silver, and costly stones symbolize? It is well to examine this subject in view of the serious possibilities implicit in the passage. What will be taken into account in the assessment?

1. Our testimony for Christ (Phil. 2:16).
2. Our suffering for Christ (1 Pet. 4:13).
3. Our faithfulness to Christ (Lk. 12:42-43; Rev. 2:10).
4. Our service for Christ (1 Cor. 3:8; Heb. 6:10).
5. Our generosity for Christ (2 Cor. 9:6; 1 Tim. 6:17-19).

6. Our use of time for Christ (Eph. 5:15-16; Col. 4:5).
7. Our exercise of spiritual gifts (Mt. 25:14-28; 1 Pet. 4:10).
8. Our self-discipline for Christ (1 Cor. 9:24-25).
9. Our leading of souls to Christ (1 Th. 2:19).

The awards conferred by our Lord from His umpire seat are symbolized by using the figure of crowns. (These will be discussed in the section on rewards, beginning on page 14.)

But the bema is not all joy and the winning of prizes for all believers. Paul told the Corinthian Christians that just as the stars differ in glory, so also will the saints (1 Cor. 15:41-42).

Some will be ashamed when He comes because of unfaithfulness to Him, of persistence in known sin, or of having been ashamed of Him before people. The apostle John wrote, "And now, little children, abide in Him, that when He appears, we may have confidence and not be ashamed before Him at His coming" (1 Jn. 2:28).

Some will suffer loss because they have used wood, hay, and straw in building on the foundation, and these materials cannot withstand fire (1 Cor. 3:12). As F. E. Marsh has said:

They have built the material of earth's products upon the foundation of Christ's being and work. The gold of Christ's deity, the silver of His vicarious sacrifice, and the precious stones of His peerless worth and coming glory are truths that

*will stand the tests of God's fire; but the wood of
self-esteem, the hay of man's frailty, and the straw
of human eloquence will all be burned up, although
the worker himself will be saved.*

Paul wrote, "If [any man's work] is burned up, he
will suffer loss; he himself will be saved, but only as
one escaping through the flames" (1 Cor. 3:15 NIV).

Will we be among those who receive the full
reward and have an abundant entrance into Christ's
kingdom, or will we be among those who are
ashamed and suffer loss?

What will the second coming mean to Christ?

Jesus said, "Father, I desire that they also whom
You gave me may be with Me where I am, that
they may behold My glory which you have given
Me; for You loved Me before the foundation of the
world" (Jn. 17:24).

The inherent selfishness of even the regener-
ated human heart is disclosed by our tendency to
think of the Lord's return more in terms of what
it will mean to us—how the accompanying events
will affect us—than of what it will mean to Him. A
very popular hymn of a generation ago epitomizes
that sentiment. Charles Gabriel wrote:

> O that will be glory for me,
> Glory for me, glory for me;
> When by His grace
> I shall look on His face,
> That will be glory,
> be glory for me!

We are rightly thrilled at the thought of our magnificent inheritance in Christ, but are we equally thrilled at the thought of His inheritance in us? Here is Paul's prayer: "I pray also that the eyes of your heart may be enlightened in order that you may know the hope to which He has called you, the riches of His glorious inheritance in the saints, and His incomparably great power for us who believe" (Eph. 1:18-19 NIV).

What thought have we given to His glorious inheritance in us? Do we pay sufficient attention to His eager expectation and anticipation of His wedding day? Is His coronation day prominent in our minds?

A. J. Janvrin wrote:

> He is waiting
> with long patience
> For His crowning day,
> For that Kingdom
> which shall never
> Pass away,
> Watching till His
> royal banner
> Floateth far and wide,
> Till He seeth of
> His travail,
> Satisfied!

Consider the startling contrast between His first coming and His second. Then He came in poverty and humiliation; soon He will come with incredible riches and glory. Then He came in weakness; soon He will come in great power. Then He came in loneliness; soon He will come accompanied by His hosts of angels and the company of the redeemed. Then He came as a man of sorrows; soon He will come with radiant and unalloyed joy. Then in mockery men placed a reed in His hand; soon He will wield the scepter of universal dominion. Then men pressed a crown of acanthus thorns upon His brow; soon He will come adorned with the many diadems He has won. Then He was blasphemed, denied, betrayed; soon every knee will bow to Him, acknowledging Him as King of kings and Lord of lords.

In His prayer to His Father, Christ made only one personal request: "I desire that they also whom You gave me may be with Me where I am, that they may behold My glory" (Jn. 17:24). This prayer reveals the deep yearning of His heart. These failing men meant a great deal to Him—and so do we. When He comes again, this yearning will have its fulfillment: "And thus we shall be with the Lord always" (1 Th. 4:17). But in the light of His greatness and majesty and holiness, do we not cry out with the psalmist in amazed wonder, "What is man that You are mindful of him, and the son of man that You visit him?" (Ps. 8:4).

When He comes again, He will be fully satisfied with the outcome of His so costly sacrifice: "After the suffering of His soul, He will . . . be satisfied" (Isa. 53:11 NIV). He will then experience the consummation of "the joy that was set before Him" (Heb. 12:2).

The noted Rabbi Duncan of Edinburgh once preached on the text "He will see His offspring" (Isa. 53:10). He divided the text as follows:

- He shall see them born and brought in.
- He shall see them educated and brought up.
- He shall see them supported and brought through.
- He shall see them glorified and brought home.

This is part of the joy set before Him.

Christ's return will result in His eternal union with His bride, the church, which He purchased with His own blood. For Him, as for us, that will mean the ecstatic joy of the wedding supper of the Lamb and eternal fellowship and communion.

When He returns, it will be to receive the kingdom of which He spoke so much on earth. When He first came to His own people and offered Himself as their king, their response was, "We don't want this man to be our king" (Lk. 19:14 NIV). But at last His kingship will be universally acknowledged and confessed. Frances Ridley Havergal wrote:

O the joy
to see Thee reigning,
Thee, my own beloved Lord!
Every tongue
Thy name confessing,
Worship, honor,
glory, blessing,
Brought to Thee
with one accord;

Thee my Master
and my Friend,
Vindicated and enthroned,
Unto earth's remotest end
Glorified, adored,
and owned.

What will the second coming mean to Satan?

The apostle John wrote, "Now have come the salvation and the power and the kingdom of our God, and the authority of His Christ. For the accuser of our brothers, who accuses them before our God day and night, has been hurled down" (Rev. 12:10 NIV).

For no one will the return of Christ have greater and more far-reaching significance than for Satan, the evil prince of this world. Scripture presents a consistent picture of two rival kingdoms confronting each other on the world scene—the kingdoms of Satan and darkness and the kingdom of God and light. Satan and his minions are allied with evil people in their plan to smash the kingdom of God and bring about the ruin of the human race.

At the end of the age, Satan is seen in alliance with the beast and the false prophet. These three, united in a common purpose to defeat Christ and secure domination of the whole world, form a sinister trinity of evil. While on earth, Jesus inflicted a stunning defeat on Satan—first in the temptation in the desert, but preeminently in His death on the cross. Christ "shared in the same, that through death He might destroy him who had the power of death, that is, the devil, and release those who through fear of death were all their lifetime subject to bondage " (Heb. 2:14-15).

It was for this very purpose that Christ the Son of God came to earth the first time: "He who does what is sinful is of the devil, because the devil has been sinning from the beginning. The reason the Son of God appeared was to destroy the devil's work" (1 Jn. 3:8 NIV).

At Calvary that victory was achieved gloriously, and the sentence of doom was passed. The blessed result was that "having disarmed the powers and authorities, He made a public spectacle of them, triumphing over them by the cross" (Col. 2:15 NIV).

Ever since Calvary, the vaunted power of the adversary has been shattered. His power is not inherent, it is derived. He is not invincible but vulnerable. He is not triumphant but doomed. He and his accomplices are reserved for a final and future judgment, which is described in Revelation 20:7-10.

When the thousand years are over, Satan will be released from his prison and will go out to deceive the nations in the four corners of the earth—Gog and Magog—to gather them for battle. . . . They marched across the breadth of the earth and surrounded the camp of God's people, the city He loves. But fire came down from heaven and devoured them. And the devil, who deceived them, was thrown into the lake of burning sulfur, where the beast and the false prophet had been thrown. They will be tormented day and night for ever and ever (NIV).

So one of the blessed absences from heaven will be Satan the tempter, the accuser, the deceiver. There will be no more temptations. We will have no weak spots of our nature. No more raking up of old sins and unfounded accusations. No more deceptions playing on our ignorance and credulity. Nothing unclean or defiling will ever enter the gates of heaven. Hallelujah!

Rewards & Resurrection Bodies

In his book *The Future Life*, Rene Pache wrote,

> Here is a searching word—the motive of our work is what counts. In that day God will test everything by His standard of truth, and if it meets with His approval, a reward will be given. The reward is not salvation, for salvation is of grace, altogether apart from works (Eph. 2:8-9). But this reward is for faithful service, because of salvation.
>
> We will have bodies fit for the full life of God to indwell and express itself forever. We will be able to eat but will not need to. We will be able to move rapidly through space and matter. We will be ageless and not know pain, tears, sorrow, sickness, or death. We will have bodies of splendor.
>
> In a promise to the Old Testament saints, the Lord compared our glorious bodies to the

shining of the moon and stars (Dan. 12:3).
Christ's glorified body is described as shining
like the sun in its strength.

Who will receive rewards?

Jesus said, "Blessed are you when men hate you,
and when they exclude you, and revile you and cast
out your name as evil, for the Son of Man's sake.
Rejoice in that day and leap for joy! For indeed
your reward is great in heaven" (Lk. 6:22-23).

"The whole subject of rewards for the believer
in heaven is one that seems to be thought of only
seldom by the ordinary Christian, or even by the
average student of the Scriptures. It is at once both
a joyous and a solemn theme, and should serve as
a potent incentive for holiness of life." So wrote
Wilbur M. Smith many years ago, and circumstances have changed little since then with regard
to this topic.

There are spiritual teachers who regard the
whole concept of rewards for service as a very
second-rate motivation. They liken it to offering
candy to a child if he will be good. But Jesus in no
way offered support to this viewpoint. In fact, He
taught the reverse. The apostle Paul also taught
about rewards in several of his letters.

No meritorious acts of ours can win salvation,
for that is a result of God's incredible and unmerited
love. But the very fact that Jesus spoke of rewards
for service on a number of occasions would indicate
that He considered their granting an important

article of faith. But in no way did He suggest or imply that service was a method of accumulating merit and thus receiving salvation. Eternal life is a gift, not a reward.

The language in which the biblical concept of rewards is expressed is highly symbolic and metaphorical and should be interpreted accordingly. Of course, faithful service will bring rewards in this life as well as in the life to come. Both are mentioned in the following verse: "'I tell you the truth,' Jesus said to them, 'no one who has left home or wife or brothers or parents or children for the sake of the kingdom of God will fail to receive many times as much in this age and, in the age to come, eternal life'" (Lk. 18:29-30 NIV).

The Beatitudes of the New Testament Gospels contain the Lord's promise of reward: "Blessed are you when they revile and persecute you, and say all kinds of evil against you falsely for My sake. Rejoice and be exceedingly glad, for great is your reward in heaven" (Mt. 5:11-12). This reward is for the person who endures slander and persecution for the sake of the Lord.

The New Testament closes with the Lord's assurance, "Behold, I am coming quickly! My reward is with Me, to give to every one according to his work" (Rev. 22:12).

Since Jesus said that the reward for affliction suffered for His sake is great and is a cause for rejoicing, we should take His words seriously and not dismiss them carelessly as some do.

Paul is equally definite on this point: "For we must all appear before the judgment seat of Christ, that each one may receive the things done in the body, according to what he has done, whether good or bad" (2 Cor. 5:10). From this passage we learn that our past deeds will confront us at the judgment seat, but it is equally clear that the salvation of the believer is not at issue at that place of judgment. That important matter was settled forever at the cross, when our substitute graciously bore the judgment that was justly due to us for our sins. As a result of that blessed event, Paul assured believers, "Through Him [Christ] everyone who believes is justified from everything you could not be justified from by the law of Moses" (Acts 13:39 NIV). The blessed consequence is, "There is therefore no condemnation to those who are in Christ Jesus" (Rom. 8:1).

So the believer doesn't need to fear that he will lose eternal life at the judgment seat. But someone might object, "Didn't Paul have a fear of being a castaway?" When Paul wrote of that possibility, it was not because he was in fear of losing his salvation. The word *castaway*, as it is rendered in the King James Version of 1 Corinthians 9:27, is better rendered "disqualified." Paul was speaking in the context of competing in the Isthmian games. The fear he entertained was that, after having exhorted others how to run so as to win the coveted prize, he himself might be disqualified for the victor's crown. After all, eternal life is not a reward but a gift.

All true believers who stand before the judgment

seat will qualify for heaven, but not all will receive the same reward. Someone once said, "Rewards will be calculated more on the basis of fidelity and suffering rather than on successful ventures." We are strongly exhorted, however, to "watch out that you do not lose what you have worked for, but that you may be rewarded fully" (2 Jn. 8 NIV).

In the parables of the minas (Lk. 19:11-27) and the talents (Mt. 25:14-30), Jesus taught that each believer has differing abilities and capacities. That is something over which we have no control and for which we are not responsible. The parable of the minas teaches that where there is equal ability but unequal faithfulness, there will be a smaller reward. On the other hand, the parable of the talents tells us that where there is unequal ability but equal faithfulness, the rewards will be the same. Christ's judgment and the reward bestowed will be according to the use we made of the opportunities given to us.

These parables, and indeed the whole subject of rewards for service, underline the importance of how we act here and now. It is now that we are determining our future status and reward in heaven. Charles Wesley wrote the following:

In hope of that
immortal crown,
I now the cross sustain
And gladly wander
up and down,
And smile at toil and pain;
I suffer out

my threescore years,
Till my Deliverer come,
And wipe away
His servant's tears,
And take His exile home.

What do the promised crowns signify?

The apostle Paul wrote, "There is laid up for
me the crown of righteousness" (2 Tim. 4:8). The
rewards promised in heaven are sometimes rep-
resented by the symbol of a crown. In the Greek
culture a crown might be either an ornamental
headdress worn by a king or queen or a wreath worn
as a symbol of victory.

Before considering the significance of the crown
awarded to victors, we should have a clear conception of the nature of heaven's rewards, for we are
apt to equate them with our earthly reward system—equal pay for equal work. The idea of merit is
thus involved. But a heavenly crown is not a matter
of quid pro quo. In the heavenly rewards, merit is
expressly excluded. Our Lord's word to His disciples
makes this clear:

*And which of you, having a servant plowing or
tending sheep, will say to him when he as come
in from the field, "Come at once and sit down to
eat"? But will he not rather say to him, "Prepare
something for my supper, and gird yourself and
serve me till I have eaten and drunk, and afterward
you will eat and drink"? Does he thank that servant
because he did the things that were commanded him?*

*I think not. So likewise you, when you have done
all those things which you are commanded, say,
"We are unprofitable servants. We have done what
was our duty to do" (Lk. 17:7-10).*

Heaven's rewards are all a matter of God's
grace. They are God's generous recognition of self-
less and sacrificial service. G. Campbell Morgan
goes so far as to assert that service for reward is not
Christian, but un-Christian! "He emptied Himself.
He served 'for the joy set before Him.' Yes, but
what was that joy? The joy of lifting other people
and blessing them" (*The Gospel Of Luke*, p.197).

The fact that the laborer who was hired to
work only at the eleventh hour received the same
wage as the one who had worked all day under-
lines the fact that most of the wage he received
was not earned, but was a generous gift from the
master. When one of the fulltime laborers charged
his master with unfairness, he replied:

*Friend, I am doing you no wrong. Did you not
agree with me for a denarius? Take what is yours
and go your way. I wish to give to this last man
the same as to you. Is it not lawful for me to do
what I wish with my own things? Or is your eye
evil because I am good?* (MT. 20:13-15).

We are not told precisely what form the crowns
in heaven will take, but John MacArthur Jr.'s view
has much to commend it: "Believers' rewards aren't
something you wear on your head like a crown. . . .
Your reward in heaven will be your capacity for ser-

vice in heaven. . . . Heaven's crowns are what we will experience, eternal life, eternal joy, eternal service, and eternal blessedness" (*Heaven*, pp.114-115).

In the New Testament, there are two Greek words translated "crown." One is *diadema*, a royal turban worn by Persian kings. It is always the symbol of kingly or imperial dignity. It refers to the kind of crown Jesus receives. The other word is *stephanos*, the victor's crown, "a symbol of triumph in the Olympic games or some such contest—hence by metonymy, a reward or prize" (Vine). It was a crown of leaves or vines, beautifully woven. This is the word that is used to denote the rewards of heaven.

Here are the crowns mentioned in Scripture:

1. Crown Of Life. "Blessed is the man who endures temptation; for when he has been approved, he will receive the crown of life which the Lord has promised to those who love Him" (Jas. 1:12). "Be faithful until death, and I will give you the crown of life" (Rev. 2:10).

This crown is bestowed in recognition of enduring and triumphing over trial and persecution even to the point of martyrdom. The motivation must be love for Christ.

2. Crown Of Righteousness. "There is laid up for me the crown of righteousness, which the Lord, the righteous Judge, will give to me on that Day, and not to me only but also to all who have loved His appearing" (2 Tim. 4:8).

This crown is awarded to those who have

completed the Christian race with integrity, with eyes fixed on the coming Lord. It is the reward for fulfilling the ministry entrusted to one.

3. Incorruptible Crown. "They do it to obtain a perishable crown, but we for an imperishable crown" (1 Cor. 9:25).

This crown is won by those who strive for mastery, for excellence. Here Paul was using the figure of the pentathlon with its tremendous demand of physical stamina. The crown is awarded to the disciplined.

4. Crown Of Rejoicing. "For what is our hope, or joy or crown of rejoicing? Is it not even you in the presence of our Lord Jesus Christ at His coming?" (1 Th. 2:19).

This is the crown of the soul-winner. It will be cause for rejoicing when, in heaven, we meet those who have been won to Christ through our ministry. This crown is open to every believer.

5. Crown Of Glory. "Shepherd the flock of God which is among you, serving as overseers, not by compulsion but willingly, . . . and when the Chief Shepherd appears, you will receive the crown of glory that does not fade away" (1 Pet. 5:2-4).

This promised award for spiritual leaders in the church should provide strong motivation for sacrificial pastoral ministry.

None of these crowns, however, is awarded automatically. There are qualifying conditions attached to each, and it is possible to forfeit a crown through unwatchfulness. In the letter to the church at Philadelphia, the risen Lord warned the believers, "Behold, I am coming quickly! Hold fast what you have, that no one may take your crown" (Rev. 3:11). This is a contemporary warning to us as well, who are often surrounded by competing claims for our love and loyalty.

Philip Doddridge wrote:

'Tis God's
all-animating voice
That calls thee from on high,
'Tis His own hand
presents the prize
To thine aspiring eye.
That prize with peerless glories bright,
Which shall
new luster boast,
When victor's wreaths
and monarch's gems
Shall blend in common dust.
Blest Savior,
introduced by Thee
Have I my race begun;
And crowned with victory
at Thy feet
I'll lay my honors down.

What will our resurrection bodies be like?

The apostle Paul wrote, "But someone will say, 'How are the dead raised up? And with what body do they come?' Foolish one, what you sow is not made alive unless it dies. And what you sow, you do not sow that body that shall be, but mere grain . . . But God gives it a body as He pleases" (1 Cor. 15:35-38).

Paul did not go into detail about the exact nature of the resurrection body of the believer, probably because of the small number of revealed facts. Yet he did make several very definite statements. About such subjects the philosopher and the scientist can make only educated guesses. With the inspired Word in our hands, however, we have certainty.

1. *It will be a spiritual body* (1 Cor. 15:44), and will be perfectly adapted to our heavenly environment.

2. *It will be a real body*, not a phantom, but will be like that of the risen Christ, who challenged His disciples, "Handle Me and see" (Lk. 24:39).

3. *It will be a recognizable body*, having identity with the physical body that has been laid to rest. After the resurrection, Jesus spoke of having "flesh and bones" (Lk. 24:39). The apostles recognized Jesus.

To clarify the issue, Paul then proceeded in 1 Corinthians 15 to draw comparisons and contrasts between the physical and the spiritual bodies.

4. *It will be a corrupt body* (v.42). It will be deathless, not subject to decay.

5. *It will be a glorious body* (v.43), no longer the body that is "sown in weakness," subject to the tyranny of sin and the attacks of Satan.

6. *It will be a powerful body* (v.43), having thrown off the frailty of its mortality.

While now the body is only an imperfect vehicle of the spirit and often frustrates it, in heaven the new body will be perfectly suited to conditions in its new sphere. "Just as we have borne the likeness of the earthly man, so shall we bear the likeness of the Man from heaven" (1 Cor. 15:49 NIV).

It should be noted that the term *spiritual body* does not imply that it is ethereal and ghostly, but rather that it will be subject to the human spirit, not to our fleshly desires. In addition, the spiritual body will be better able to express the believer's aspirations than the earthly body can.

There are two current misconceptions about the spiritual body that need correction: (a) That it will be identical with the body that was buried. (b) That there is no organic connection between the body that was buried and that which is raised. If these conceptions were so, there would need to be a new creation, not a resurrection. We must acknowledge that there is mystery here, mystery that will be revealed only in heaven.

In answering the question, "With what kind of body will they come?" Paul enunciated four truths, which are illustrated in the growth of a seed and in the diversity of animals and of the sun, moon, and stars.

1. *What grows from the seed we sow is not altogether identical with what is sown* (1 Cor. 15:37). An acorn produces not an acorn but an oak, yet both enjoy the same life force.

2. *Each kind of seed has a distinctive, God-given body* (Gen. 1:11; 1 Cor. 15:38).

3. *The fruit of the seed sown has an organic connection with the seed from which it sprang.* It is not a new creation but is the product of something already in existence.

4. *As there is great diversity in the bodies in the animal kingdom, so it will be in the heavenly kingdom* (1 Cor. 15:39-41).

If the resurrection body is not organically related to the body that is sown as it dies, there can be no resurrection. That we are unable to explain this does not alter its truth. We should keep in mind that there are other mysteries, perhaps connected, that we have to live with. Medical people tell us that in a lifetime our total body substance has been changed about 10 times, and yet our personal identities have continued; we remain the same people. Our memory of past events remains unimpaired. This is a mystery too, but it does shed some light on our problem.

In 1 Corinthians 15:42-44, Paul contrasted the old body with the new in four respects:

1. *It is sown corrupt but will be raised in incorruption* (v.42). There has been only one body not subject to corruption (Ps. 16:10; Acts 2:27). Sooner or later our physical bodies waste away. We all are victims of disease and, ultimately, death. Although the hearse is now ubiquitous, our spiritual bodies will be imperishable.

2. *It is sown in dishonor but will be raised in glory*

(v.43). There is nothing beautiful or glorious about a decaying corpse. We dispose of it with respect in a grave or by cremation. But the resurrection body will be a glorious body, inconceivably more beautiful and wonderful. This is assured because of "the Lord Jesus Christ, who will transform our lowly body that it may be conformed to His glorious body" (Phil. 3:20-21).

3. *It is sown in weakness but will be raised in power* (v.43). Bible commentator Leon Morris wrote that the strength of youth inevitably yields to the frailty of age. A dead body is a symbol of weakness, but our new body, like our Lord's, will be characterized by power. Sleep will not be necessary to relieve weariness or recoup spent energy. Our abilities will be enlarged, and we will throw off the limitations of which we are so conscious in life on earth" (*First Corinthians*, p.28).

4. *It is sown a natural body; it will be raised a spiritual body* (v.44). The natural body is adapted to life in this world but is not fitted for life in the next. The spiritual body is the organ that is intimately related to the spirit of man, just as his present body is intimately related to his earthly life. No longer will our bodies be subject to the laws that limit our physical life.

Our Lord's resurrection body is the pattern for ours (Phil. 3:20-21). He ate with His disciples (Jn. 21:9,12-13). He passed through closed doors (Jn. 20:19). He appeared and disappeared from sight. He claimed to have flesh and bones (Lk. 24:39).

In other words, there was a real connection and identity with His former body, minus some of the limitations of that body.

Our bodies are now subject to limitation and deterioration, they confine and cramp us, and they are destined to return to their constituent elements. But "we shall be changed." When our Lord returns, a glorious transformation will occur. Our lowly bodies will become like His glorious body and will be bodies in which our longings and aspirations will find perfect expression.

What was our Lord's resurrection body like?

It was certainly different from that same body before death.

1. There were three occasions when He was not recognized at first by His closest friends:

"When the morning had now come, Jesus stood on the shore; yet the disciples did not know that it was Jesus" (Jn. 21:4).

"Now when she had said this, she turned around and saw Jesus standing there, and did not know that it was Jesus" (Jn. 20:14).

"Jesus Himself drew near and went with them. But their eyes were restrained, so that they did not know Him" (Lk. 24:15-16).

2. While the Lord's resurrection body was indeed different, it bore similarities to His physical body. He said He had "flesh and bones" (Lk. 24:39). He denied that He was a ghost (Lk. 24:37-39). He prepared breakfast for His men and ate with them (Jn. 21:9-14; Lk. 24:42-43).

3. *However, He was able to pass through closed doors* (Jn. 20:19). He was no longer confined by our limitations of time and space.

4. *His was a real body.* In answer to Thomas' disbelief, He extended the invitation, "Reach your finger here, and look at My hands" (Jn. 20:27). And to Mary, "Do not cling to Me" (v.17).

Jesus gave satisfying evidence that He was just the same person as before the cross. He was recognized by His intimates who were now prepared to die for Him—as most of them did.

It is intriguing to note that our Lord's body retained its scars in the new body. Exactly what this signifies is difficult to say. One interesting suggestion is that scars received as suffering for Christ's sake will persist in some way, not as blemishes but as eternal badges of honor.

How To Gain Entrance To Heaven

Jesus said, "I tell you the truth, unless you change and become like little children, you will never enter the kingdom of heaven" (Mt. 18:3 NIV).

The Scriptures definitely support the belief in life after death and the existence of such a place as heaven. There is no doubt that our Lord and His apostles taught these truths, and they also taught with equal clarity that there is such a place as hell, where the impenitent receive the reward of their deeds.

The popular idea, according to recent polls, is

that good people go to heaven, and a majority of those polled rated their own chances of going there to be good. There are few who don't want to go to heaven. Most base their expectation on their performance in this life, irrespective of their relationship to Christ. Is this a valid hope?

Here again we are driven to the Scriptures for an authoritative answer. All else is speculation, but in a matter of such far-reaching importance, we need more than that—we need certainty.

In a world where there is so much injustice and inequality, where the righteous suffer and the evil prosper, where the weak are exploited and the powerful flourish, it is easy to conclude as Israel did, "The way of the Lord is not fair" (Ezek. 18:25). In our contemporary society the administration of the judicial system often gives the breaks to the criminal rather than to the victim. The greater number of crimes go unpunished, while meritorious action is often unrewarded. This creates a puzzling moral problem.

The psalmist Asaph, faced with a similar problem, had no answer and almost lost his faith. Hear him:

> But as for me, my feet had almost slipped; I had nearly lost my foothold. For I envied the arrogant when I saw the prosperity of the wicked. They have no struggles; their bodies are healthy and strong. They are free from the burdens common to man; they are not plagued by human ills (PS. 73:2-5 NIV).

Because of human sin, life on earth is manifestly unjust. If God is as good and just as the Scriptures state and as we have maintained, how can He retain His character while permitting such a state of affairs to continue? If He remains inactive in this situation, it would appear that He is either uncaring or is powerless to redress the obvious injustices of this life.

But both Scripture and history are replete with affirmations that He is neither uncaring nor inactive. This life is not the end of all. Such inequalities will be redressed.

Where did Asaph discover the solution to his problem? He wrote, "Surely in vain have I kept my heart pure; in vain have I washed my hands in innocence. . . . When I tried to understand all this, it was oppressive to me till I entered the sanctuary of God; then I understood their final destiny" (vv.13,16-17 NIV). Like him, we should take our perplexing problems into the presence of God and try to see things from His perspective. It is the end-view that is important.

Scripture abounds with intimations that a day is coming when injustices will be made right and inequalities straightened out, when evil will be punished and virtue appropriately rewarded. This will take place at the day of judgment. Those who in this life have not availed themselves of the only way of salvation through the grace of God and the atoning death of Christ will not enter the gates of heaven. The Word is unequivocal: "There shall by no means enter it anything that defiles, or causes an abomination or a lie, but only those who are written in the Lamb's Book of Life" (Rev. 21:27).

What does it mean to have one's name written in the Lamb's Book of Life?

The metaphor of books of record occurs throughout Scripture, beginning with Moses' plea to God to be "blot me out" of God's book as an atonement for the sins of the people of Israel (Ex. 32:32). This figure of speech is drawn from the registers of the tribes of Israel. Its final appearance is in the text we are considering.

Concerning the judgment in front of the great white throne, we read, "Then I saw a great white throne. . . . And I saw the dead, small and great, standing before God, and books were opened. And another book was opened, which is the Book of Life. And the dead were judged according to their works, by the things which were written in the books" (Rev. 20:11-12).

One set of books, then, contains the record of each person's life-history. The other book is the Lamb's Book of Life. The first record can bring only condemnation, for all have fallen short of God's standards. In the Book of Life are recorded the names of those who have repented of their sins and exercised saving faith in Christ as Redeemer and Savior.

Remember that it's our decision whether or not our names are written there. John Bunyan in his *Pilgrim's Progress* describes the armed man who came up to the table where the man with the book and the inkhorn was seated, and said, "Set down my name." It is open to anyone to do just that.

A living faith in Christ, "the Lamb of God who takes away the sin of the world" (Jn. 1:29), is the sole condition for having our names written in that book, and that constitutes our passport through the pearly gates. "They that trust in Jesus Christ," writes Alexander Maclaren, "shall have their names written in the Book of Life; graven on the High Priest's breastplate, and inscribed on His mighty hand and His faithful heart."

Why not make absolutely certain of heaven by opening your heart to Christ the Savior and Lord right now, inviting Him to enter, to cleanse it from sin, and to make it His permanent dwelling place? He gives this assurance: "If anyone hears My voice and opens the door, I will come in to him and dine with him, and he with Me" (Rev. 3:20).

Note to the Reader

This chapter, "Just Before Heaven: The Judgment Seat Of Christ," is based on a portion of the book *Heaven: Better By Far*, written by the late J. Oswald Sanders. He was putting the finishing touches on the manuscript of this book about heaven when he went home to be with the Lord. He went quietly in his sleep a week after his 90th birthday.

Dr. Sanders was one of the last of a great generation of Bible teachers, and we are the richer for having been the heirs of his ministry for 70 years.

He wrote more than 40 books and preached thousands of times. His ministry spanned the world, and he was loved by all who knew him.

Dr. Sanders' book *Heaven: Better By Far* is available from Discovery House Publishers.

Four

OUR ETERNAL HOME

Home. What a wonderful word. It speaks of love and warmth and family. Who wouldn't want to live forever in a place that can be called "home"? Heaven is just such a place. It will be home to all who have put their faith and trust in the Lord Jesus Christ, and it will be a place of unimaginable joys. Most important, it will be the place where we will have forever fellowship with God the Father, God the Son, and God the Holy Spirit. It will be a home like no other, and we will live a life that far surpasses even our best day on earth. Join my father, Richard De Haan, as he provides a clear portrait of heaven—our eternal home.

—*Martin R. De Haan II*

God's Dwelling Place And Ours

The mention of the word *heaven* raises at once a number of questions. Is there really such a place? If so, where is it? What is heaven like? Will everyone go there, or just a certain privileged few? And then, some will ask, "Do we go there immediately at death, or does the soul 'sleep' for a while?"

For many people in this first part of the twenty-first century, these questions are not relevant. They scoff at the idea of life after death and ridicule belief in a heaven of eternal bliss and a hell of everlasting punishment. They are convinced that man's existence ends at the grave.

Christians do believe in a beautiful place called heaven, and they look forward to eternal life within its gates. Based on their faith in God's Word, they anticipate the joys that await them in their eternal home. This comforting thought brings healing to the wounds of their earthly existence and quenches their sorrows.

The place to find out about heaven is the Bible. The word *heaven* in its singular and plural forms occurs more than 600 times in Scripture. We are given much information about our eternal home, and in this lesson we will consider it carefully in two aspects: (1) the habitation of God and (2) the home of departed saints.

■ THE HABITATION OF GOD

The Bible often speaks of heaven as God's "habitation" and explicitly declares that He dwells there.

> *Thus says the High and Lofty One who inhabits eternity, whose name is Holy: "I dwell in the high and holy place, with him who has a contrite and humble spirit, to revive the spirit of the humble, and to revive the heart of the contrite ones"* (ISA. 57:15).

Solomon also recognized heaven as God's home when he prayed:

> *May You hear the supplication of Your servant and of Your people Israel, when they pray toward this place. Hear in heaven Your dwelling place; and when You hear, forgive* (1 KI. 8:30).

This does not mean that God is absent from earth. His presence is everywhere, but His dwelling place is in heaven. He abides there, and from that location He is present throughout all His creation.

The Bible also teaches that heaven is the location of God's throne. The psalmist declared:

> *The Lord has established His throne in heaven, and His kingdom rules over all* (PS. 103:19).

God is king of the universe He created; the Bible speaks of "His throne," which He occupies in heaven. From there He rules over the affairs of men. Nebuchadnezzar, the mighty king of Babylon, learned of God's sovereign rulership through firsthand experience. He had become self-centered and proud, and the Lord had temporarily chastened him by a period of severe mental illness. When it was all over, he prayed:

> *Now I, Nebuchadnezzar, praise and extol and
> honor the King of heaven, all of whose works are
> truth, and His ways justice. And those who walk
> in pride He is able to put down* (DAN. 4:37).

God, the Almighty King, rules in majesty over
His entire creation. He holds all things together
by His mighty power. He may permit evil men
and the rulers of darkness to have their day, but
He has not lost control of the world—not for one
moment! Although the wicked may rebel against
His laws and declare themselves masters of their
own destiny, God from heaven is still in com-
mand.

Psalm 2 describes the empty efforts of the
nations to rebel against the Lord God and against
His Christ. These boasters say:

> *Let us break Their bonds in pieces and cast away
> Their cords from us* (v.3).

But the psalmist went on to express the folly
and madness of seeking to stand up against the
Almighty:

> *He who sits in the heavens shall laugh; the Lord
> shall hold them in derision. Then He shall speak to
> them in His wrath, and distress them in His deep
> displeasure* (vv.4-5).

Yes, God in heaven has only to speak the word,
and all His enemies will be destroyed. When the

Bible speaks of heaven as God's throne, therefore, it means that this is the center of His administration, the seat of His authority, the place from which He issues His edicts, commands, and sovereign decrees.

The Bible also teaches that God accepts our worship and hears our prayers in heaven. The Lord told Solomon at the finishing of the temple:

If My people who are called by My name will humble themselves, and pray and seek My face, and turn from their wicked ways, then I will hear from heaven, and will forgive their sin and heal their land (2 CHR. 7:14).

King David, the father of Solomon, had also learned that God hears the prayers of His people. David had earnestly sought God's help, and the Lord had granted him victory over the Philistines. In gratitude he wrote:

In my distress I called upon the Lord, and criedout to my God; He heard my voice from His temple, and my cry entered His ears (2 SAM. 22:7).

God has promised to listen to the prayers of His people. What a blessing that the same is true for Christians today! Whether we want to confess our sins to Him or just to praise Him, He will hear and respond.

In heaven, God not only accepts the worship of His people on earth, but He also receives the adoration of the heavenly hosts who dwell there with Him. In Hebrews 12:22, for example, we are told of an innumerable company of angels who abide in heaven. The Bible portrays them as constantly worshiping and serving God. They are continually going back and forth, from earth to heaven and from heaven to earth, fulfilling the Lord's instructions.

Are they not all ministering spirits sent forth to minister for those who will inherit salvation? (HEB. 1:14).

All of this activity centers around God's throne. There they receive their orders, and there they return when their mission is accomplished.

Other angelic beings, the cherubim and seraphim, are with God in heaven. Creatures of service and worship, they attend His throne to extol His virtues, to guard His holiness, and to render praise through obedience.

Heaven is the habitation of God. From there He rules over all creation, hears the prayers of His people, and accepts the worship of His earthly subjects and His heavenly attendants.

■ THE HOME OF DEPARTED SAINTS

Not only is heaven God's habitation, but it is also the place where His saints will dwell forever. We can rightly call heaven "our eternal home." Death does not end all; the soul lives on. And for the believer, the soul at death immediately enters forever into the presence of God.

Some false religionists teach otherwise. They

refer to those who die as being "asleep," and by this they mean that their souls cease to exist until some time of future resurrection. But the term *soul sleep*, as used in this manner, is a misnomer—simply because a soul with no existence apart from the body could not be referred to as "sleeping." If it doesn't exist it's gone! This means that at some future time God would find it necessary to re-create the entire individual. The body would first have to be resurrected; then it would need to be given a new soul. This is contrary to the teaching of God's Word.

Death involves physical and spiritual separation—not annihilation! Physical death occurs when the soul is separated from the body. Spiritual death is the eternal separation of the soul from God. Although the believer in Christ may die physically, having his soul separated from his body, he can never die spiritually. He will never experience the separation of his soul from God.

My believing friend, this should be a special comfort to you. It means that your Christian loved ones who have died are not separated from the Lord and never will be. When they gave their hearts to Christ, they received life everlasting. Jesus said:

He who hears My word and believes in Him who sent Me has everlasting life (JN. 5:24).

Those who have died in Christ have entered into the presence of God, and even now they abide with Him in heaven. Jesus taught this truth in His words to Martha at the time of the resurrection of

Lazarus. When Jesus arrived at Bethany, four days after Lazarus had died, Martha came out to meet Him and complained, "Lord, if You had been here, my brother would not have died" (Jn. 11:21). Then Christ, assuring Martha that her brother would rise again, stated this beautiful, comforting truth:

I am the resurrection and the life. He who believes in Me, though he may die, he shall live. And whoever lives and believes in Me shall never die (vv.25-26).

We may learn two important lessons from these words of Christ. First, even though believers may die physically, as Lazarus did, their bodies will someday be resurrected. Remember, Jesus said, "I am the resurrection and the life." Second, through faith in Christ the child of God possesses eternal life. Therefore, in the deepest sense of the word, he will never die. That's why Jesus could give the glorious promise, "Whoever lives and believes in Me shall never die."

Yes, the body may perish, but the soul of the Christian lives on—never to be separated from God, the source of life. Those who teach that the soul of man ceases to exist at death deny a clear statement from the lips of our Lord Himself. Remember that Jesus said, "Whoever lives and believes in Me *shall never die.*"

■ IN CHRIST'S PRESENCE

When the believer dies, he departs from this life to go immediately into the presence of Christ. At the moment physical life is ended, therefore, the

Christian meets Jesus face to face in his eternal home in heaven. The words of the Lord Jesus at Calvary emphasize this truth. As Christ hung on the accursed tree, one of the dying thieves expressed faith in Him, crying out, "Lord, remember me when You come into Your kingdom" (Lk. 23:42). The Lord Jesus gave His word that they would meet again, and not way off in the far distant future. He promised, "*Today* you will be *with* Me in Paradise" (v.43).

The apostle Paul viewed the period between death and resurrection as a time of joy, blessing, and fellowship in the presence of Christ. He told the believers in Philippi:

> *For to me, to live is Christ, and to die is gain. But if I live on in the flesh, this will mean fruit from my labor; yet what I shall choose I cannot tell. For I am hard pressed between the two, having a desire to depart and be with Christ, which is far better* (PHIL. 1:21-23).

It's plain to see that the apostle fully expected to be with the Lord the very moment he departed from this life. Because of this he could say, "To die is gain" and "to depart and be with Christ . . . is far better."

In 2 Corinthians 5:6-8, he expressed again his sincere conviction that the day he would leave this body, he would join his Savior in heaven:

> *So we are always confident, knowing that while we are at home in the body we are absent from the*

Lord. For we walk by faith, not by sight. We are confident, yes, well pleased rather to be absent from the body and to be present with the Lord.

To give proper emphasis to the tenses used in the Greek, this last verse should read, "We are confident, I say, and willing, rather to be once-for-all away from home as far as the body is concerned, and to be once-for-all at home with the Lord."

Paul was not speaking here about the resurrection of the body. That will occur when the trumpet sounds for the rapture of the church. Rather, he spoke of what happens to the soul immediately following death. When a Christian dies, his soul is ushered into Christ's presence in heaven. Death for the believer brings about an immediate, once-for-all change—from being in our body on earth to being with our Lord in our eternal home.

This is the fulfillment of Jesus' prayer of John 17, spoken shortly before His crucifixion:

Father, I desire that they also whom You gave Me may be with Me where I am, that they may behold My glory which You have given Me; for You loved Me before the foundation of the world (v.24).

For the believer, this prayer finds fulfillment at death. He enters heaven and begins to experience all the wonderful blessings of being with the Lord.

■ SUMMARY

In this lesson we have emphasized two important truths. First, heaven is the habitation of God. It's where the Lord rules over all His creation, accepts the worship of His beings, and hears our prayers. Second, heaven is the home of departed saints, where we will abide forever in the presence of our Savior, the Lord Jesus Christ. Although our bodies may be buried in the grave to be resurrected at the rapture of the church, our souls go immediately to be with the Lord.

Not everyone, however, will enjoy the glories of heaven. There is one condition that must be met if you are to enter that eternal home. The only condition is faith in God's Son, the Lord Jesus Christ. He said:

> *For God so loved the world that He gave His only begotten Son, that whoever believes in Him should not perish but have everlasting life (JN. 3:16).*

The Holy City

I am sure many Americans who visit our capital city, Washington, DC, are as impressed as I was when they view its magnificent structures and monuments. A walk down the Federal Mall, going past the Art Institute and Smithsonian Institution, the towering Washington Monument, the majestic White House, and standing finally in a moment of reflection at the Lincoln Memorial is a thrilling experience. As Americans we can be proud, in the right sense of the word, of our national capital! It ranks with the great cities of the world—London,

Paris, Tokyo, or Rome—in beauty and splendor.

Yet, every Christian is a citizen of a heavenly city—a city more dazzling and beautiful than anyone on earth has ever seen. Its streets shimmer with gold and its jeweled walls and foundations glow in a spectrum of color. We are told that it is free from evil of all kinds, and nothing in it will ever tarnish or decay.

You see, a day is coming when our present solar system will be burned with fire and will be replaced by a new heaven and a new earth. Peter wrote:

> *But the day of the Lord will come as a thief in the night, in which the heavens will pass away with a great noise, and the elements will melt with fervent heat; both the earth and the works that are in it will be burned up* (2 PET. 3:10).

According to this prophecy, our universe will be shattered with a mighty roaring sound. It will burst into flames with such intense heat that even the elements that make up matter will be dissolved. The sun, the moon, the planets, and the distant stars will all be engulfed in flame, but this will not be a tragedy. It will not mean annihilation but transformation.

The Word of God declares that out of the ruins will emerge a glorious new world—our eternal home. The apostle John saw it in a vision, and under the inspiration of the Holy Spirit described the scene:

> *Now I saw a new heaven and a new earth, for the first heaven and the first earth had passed away.*

Also there was no more sea. Then I, John, saw the
holy city, New Jerusalem, coming down out of
heaven from God, prepared as a bride adorned for
her husband (REV. 21:1-2).

The New Jerusalem, which John proceeded to describe, will rest upon the great planet that will come into existence. This holy city that comes down will be the capital of the new heaven and new earth. It is called the "New Jerusalem" to distinguish it from the two other Jerusalems mentioned in the Bible—the earthly city still in Palestine today and the "heavenly Jerusalem" of Hebrews 12. (The heavenly Jerusalem and the New Jerusalem are actually the same city, but seen at different stages of redemptive history.)

Let's now consider three aspects of this heavenly city, the eternal home of the redeemed: (1) its present location, (2) its place in the coming millennial reign of Christ, and (3) its external appearance as it comes down to rest upon the great planet of the future.

■ THE LOCATION OF THE HEAVENLY CITY

The eternal home of the saints is now in heaven as the capital city, which is implied in the name "the heavenly Jerusalem" (Heb. 12:22). But this raises a question that has often been asked, "Where is heaven?"

Some think it is located somewhere in the northern skies. To support this, they point out that astronomers have discovered only one area in space that appears to be empty—the region around the North Star. No other stars have ever been discovered there. Rather, only a faint luminous glow has been detected. Therefore, they speculate that this must be the location of heaven.

For biblical evidence to support their position, they point to Psalm 75, which reads in part:

For exaltation comes neither from the east nor from the west nor from the south (v.6).

They reason that if "exaltation" does not originate from the east, west, or south, it can come only from the north. Thus they conclude that since God is the One who gives blessing, this verse teaches that His throne is located somewhere in the north. In addition, they point out that the altar sacrifice was the brightness of God's glory coming from the north (Ezek. 1:4).

These scriptural affirmations may give us a hint as to the present location of heaven and its capital city, though we can't be sure that it is in some distant place out in space. It may be much nearer to earth than we think, and we need not be disturbed by statements of unbelievers who say that no astronomers have ever seen evidence of its existence. The fact is that vast reaches in space have not yet been probed by the most powerful telescopes. Besides, it is foolish to deny that something exists just because it cannot be seen with the eyes or detected by our present equipment. Every scientifically minded person realizes that something may be very real while being completely imperceptible to us.

We believe beyond all doubt in the existence of a glorious city called "the heavenly Jerusalem." We are confident that the saints of past ages and our loved ones who died in Christ are there now, and that we will someday join them. The patriarchs looked forward to entering this promised city when they died. Abraham left his homeland, an area of well-established cities, to follow the call of God, though he did not know his earthly destination. Nevertheless he was able to exercise great faith and patience while living as a wanderer because "he waited for the city which has foundations, whose builder and maker is God" (Heb. 11:10).

Even though Abraham, Isaac, and Jacob were never able to gain full possession of the Promised Land, they did not despair. They realized that a heavenly city was awaiting them. That's the reason the Bible says that "now they desire a better, that is, a heavenly country. Therefore God is not ashamed to be called their God, for He has prepared a city for them" (Heb. 11:16).

This heavenly city, planned and built by God, is mentioned again in Hebrews 12.

> *But you have come to Mount Zion and to the city of the living God, the heavenly Jerusalem, to an innumerable company of angels* (HEB. 12:22).

I repeat, then, that today the great city of God for which Abraham looked is in heaven, the dwelling place of the souls of all believers in Christ who have died. We do not know exactly where heaven with its capital city is located, but we wait for it with hopeful anticipation.

■ ITS PLACE IN THE MILLENNIAL KINGDOM

What will be the location of the heavenly city during the millennial reign of Christ? Some believe that throughout the coming golden age it will be suspended above the earth as a satellite city. While this theory cannot be proven, there is some evidence to substantiate it.

In the first place, the Scriptures indicate that Christ and His glorified saints will rule the earth during the millennial age. Our Lord is depicted as reigning from Jerusalem accompanied by resurrected believers. This does not mean, of course, that the glorified saints will be subjected to the limitations of earthly life. Their home will be the heavenly Jerusalem, but they will serve in certain capacities here. Dr. Alva J. McClain explained it this way:

> The residence of the saints in heaven while ruling on earth, actually, is much less of a problem than that of a businessman whose office is in a city while his residence is in the suburbs.

A number of Bible scholars believe that during the tribulation period, which comes just before the establishment of the millennial kingdom, the heavenly Jerusalem will become visible to earth dwellers. This would be in perfect keeping with the fact that miracles of power will be on open display. Furthermore, in Revelation 13:6 we may have a hint that the people on earth will be able to see the heavenly Jerusalem. We read:

Then he opened his mouth in blasphemy against God, to blaspheme His name, His tabernacle, and those who dwell in heaven.

The Greek text does not contain the word *and*, which we find in our English version. It should read, "Then he opened his mouth for blasphemies against God, to blaspheme His name, and His tabernacle—those who dwell in heaven." Could it be that the sight of this satellite city where the saints dwell triggers this blasphemy?

Another indication that the heavenly Jerusalem will be relatively near the earth is found in Paul's description of the rapture and resurrection at Christ's coming for His own. He told the Thessalonian believers that the meeting place will be "in the air."

The Lord Himself will descend from heaven with a shout, with the voice of an archangel, and with the trumpet of God. And the dead in Christ will rise first. Then we who are alive and remain shall be caught up together with them in the clouds to meet the Lord in the air. And thus we shall always be with the Lord (1 TH. 4:16-17).

The place where the Lord and His saints will meet in the air could be the location from which they will share with Christ in His rule over the earth during those 1,000 years. If this is true, and the heavenly Jerusalem is a satellite city suspended above the earth, the resurrected and translated saints would have ready access to earth from their dwelling place above. This would facilitate their ruling with Christ, as promised in the Word of God.

A further implication that during the millennial age the heavenly Jerusalem will be a satellite city is found in John's description, which we read earlier, as he saw it descending from heaven (Rev. 21:2). The language used indicates that this city was already in existence before it made its descent to earth. When we recall that Hebrews 12 depicts the "heavenly Jerusalem" as a home of "the spirits of just men made perfect" (v.23), we have good reason to believe that the eternal home of the resurrected believers will be the same city. We find it logical to think of it in three stages: (1) the heavenly Jerusalem where the spirits of the dead now live, (2) the satellite city from which certain believers commute to earth during the millennial age, and (3) the settled city which will ultimately rest upon "a new earth."

■ ITS GENERAL DESCRIPTION

John described graphically the coming of the New Jerusalem to the earth. Remember, our entire present solar system will have been dissolved into one great mass by God's fire of judgment, and the new heavens and new earth will have been built out of its ruins. Then John said:

Now I saw a new heaven and a new earth, for the first heaven and the first earth had passed away.

*Also there was no more sea. Then I, John, saw
the holy city, New Jerusalem, coming down out
of heaven from God, prepared as a bride adorned
for her husband. And I heard a loud voice from
heaven saying, "Behold, the tabernacle of God is
with men, and He will dwell with them, and they
shall be His people. God Himself will be with them
and be their God" (REV. 21:1-3).*

What a breathtaking sight this must have
been! And how awesome the voice that declared
the glorious truth that God will forever dwell
there with His people! As John looked at the city
coming down, he saw it glowing with the glory
of God. He observed it resting upon its 12 jeweled foundations and rising skyward, sparkling
like a diamond in the sunlight and reflecting its
brightness over the whole earth. Then John gave
its measurements:

*He who talked with me had a gold reed to measure
the city, its gates, and its wall. The city is laid out
as a square; its length is as great as its breadth.
And he measured the city with the reed: twelve
thousand furlongs. Its length, breadth, and height
are equal (REV. 21:15-16).*

The New Jerusalem is depicted as being 1,500
miles long and wide. We also read that "its length,
breadth, and height are equal." Many Bible students believe these numbers should be taken
symbolically and that the city, cubical in form,
resembles the shape of the holy of holies in the

tabernacle and temple. There seems to be no good reason, however, to depart from the literal acceptance of the dimensions of the holy city.

Even if we take the numbers literally, though, we cannot speak with absolute certainty about its height. But if the phrase "length, breadth, and height are equal" means that the city is actually 1,500 miles high as well as wide and long, we still cannot be sure that we should take this as depicting the shape of a perfect cube or of a pyramid going up 1,500 miles. Some Bible students believe that the word *equal* in this context simply means that it will be square, and that in height it will be level.

Whether we accept the city as existing in the form of a cube, a pyramid, or a perfectly level square makes very little difference. In either case the size is most amazing. At the ground level it covers more area than India, and if placed in the United States, it would reach from the tip of Maine to the tip of Florida, and from the shore of the Atlantic Ocean westward to Denver. What a city that will be! It will rise up from the earth on 12 foundations of precious jewels and will glow with perpetual light as it reflects the glory of God and shines out through its jasper walls. What beauty! What immensity! No need for anyone to worry about whether or not there will be room for the redeemed!

Yes, glory—indescribable blessedness—will be the eternal portion of all who trust in Jesus Christ. Believers are now citizens of the heavenly Jerusalem, and someday in glorified bodies they will enter the

New Jerusalem. What a great salvation is ours! What a wonderful prospect! What a blessed hope!

The Home Of Beauty

The day is coming when a great explosion will occur and a cleansing fire will sweep across our entire planetary system. This catastrophic event will mark the end of time, the final defeat of Satan, and the ushering in of eternity. After describing the millennium, the apostle John said:

> Then I saw a great white throne and Him who sat on it, from whose face the earth and the heaven fled away. And there was found no place for them (REV. 20:11).

The apostle Peter also described this day of judgment when he wrote:

> The heavens will pass away with a great noise, and the elements will melt with fervent heat; both the earth and the works that are in it will be burned up (2 PET. 3:10).

In this manner the material of our present universe will be purged, purified, and transformed. Out of this all-encompassing conflagration will emerge a new planet, which John called "a new heaven and a new earth." The heavenly Jerusalem, where the saints of the ages now dwell with Christ will then descend from a region untouched by the flame and come to rest on the new earth, where it will remain forever as the capital city of heaven. It will then be called the New Jerusalem. The apostle John described this great event in Revelation 21.

When we think about the eternal home of all who believe in Jesus as personal Savior, some questions naturally arise: "What kind of place will it be?" "What will we do there?" Many of our questions are answered in Revelation 21 and 22. Included is a description of the beauty of the heavenly city from without and its glory within. In this chapter we will consider these two aspects of our eternal home.

■ ITS BEAUTY FROM WITHOUT

Let's imagine we're standing on a vast plain with the heavenly city towering above us in resplendent beauty. We see a brilliant, shining city, with light streaming through its jasper walls and pearly gates, and a full spectrum of color gleaming from its jeweled foundation.

Its Jasper Wall.

As we gaze in awe on the city, the first thing to attract our attention is its massive jasper wall. The apostle John described it as follows: "Her light was like a most precious stone, like a jasper stone, clear as crystal. Also she had a great and high wall" (Rev. 21:11-12). In verse 17 he said this wall measures 144 cubits in height (216 feet). Even though we may not be able to identify exactly what kind of jasper this is, we do know that these semi-precious stones are translucent in composition, so that light is able to pass through them. From these jasper walls, therefore, radiate brilliant rays of dazzling color for all to see. The glory of the city will thus be visible from afar, and even the dwellers in the area outside the walls will share in its brightness.

Although the wall around the city is real, it is also symbolic. The purpose of the wall is not to preserve the city against invaders, for God will have no enemies in the new earth. Being 216 feet high, it impressively signifies that no one will enter the city apart from God's grace. The wall is too high to be scaled by human effort, and the only portals are the 12 guarded gates. The requirement for admittance is salvation, and no one who has rejected God's plan will be able to go in. Salvation is the gift of God's grace to those who humbly acknowledge their need of forgiveness and who receive Jesus Christ as Savior.

Its Jeweled Foundations.

The next thing to catch our vision as we look at the city is its jeweled foundation. Normally, foundations undergird the walls of a city and lie below the ground where they cannot be seen. But this is not the case in the New Jerusalem, for the foundation supporting its walls is fully visible to all and is indescribably beautiful. Comprising 12 layers of different precious stones—from sapphire to emerald—the wall stretches all the way around the city.

Many Bible students believe that these jewels reflect all the colors of the rainbow, though we do not know the precise characteristics of each stone. Beginning at ground level, these were probably the colors seen by the apostle: the jasper stone may have been a light green or yellow; the sapphire, a sky-blue or azure; the chalcedony, containing a combination of colors, was mostly green and blue; the emerald, bright green; the sardonyx, red and white; the sardius, reddish in color; chrysolite, golden yellow; beryl, sea-green; topaz, yellow-green and transparent; chrysoprasus, golden-green; jacinth, violet; and amethyst, either rose-red or purple. The radiating light of the city, shining out through the jasper wall and blazing through the open gates, reflects from these precious stones in splendrous color.

The beauty of the city to the observer from the outside will be magnificent, as described in Revelation 21:19-20. In the foundation stones will be inscribed the names of the 12 apostles of the Lamb (v.14), those valiant men of Israel who first proclaimed the message of a risen Christ to the Gentile world.

Its Pearly Gates.

In the walls of the heavenly city are 12 gates of pearl, and they will never close. Here is John's description: Also she had a great and high wall with twelve gates, and twelve angels at the gates, and names written on them, which are the names of the

twelve tribes of the children of Israel . . . . The twelve
gates were twelve pearls; each individual gate was of
one pearl. And the street of the city was pure gold,
like transparent glass (REV. 21:12,21).

Some Bible scholars believe that these gates of pearl suggest salvation by grace. Even as a wound to an oyster results in the formation of a valuable pearl, the gates of heaven can be entered only because the Lord Jesus was "wounded for our transgressions" (Isa. 53:5). Although men wickedly rejected Him and crucified Him, it was through this death that salvation was made possible. Now, all who believe on Him can look forward to entering the pearly gates of heaven. Jesus Himself said, "I am the door. If anyone enters by Me, he will be saved" (Jn. 10:9).

The gates are open at all times and in every direction, for salvation is still offered freely to everyone. The angels who keep watch at the open gates, therefore, are a wonderful contrast to the cherubim who guarded the closed gate of Eden after Adam and Eve sinned. These angels keep the way of access open, while the cherubim kept the Garden closed to fallen humanity.

In the gates are inscribed the names of the 12 tribes of Israel, for "salvation is of the Jews." The Lord Jesus Christ was born of the seed of Abraham and David, and only those who come through the blessedness of His "Messianic gate" can pass through the pearly gates into heaven.

Its Beauty Within.

Having envisioned the beauty of the New Jerusalem from the outside, let us now pass through one of those pearly gates and enter the city. As we cross the threshold, we gaze in wonder, for before us lie a golden street, a crystal river, and the tree of life.

Its Golden Street.

One of the characteristics of the heavenly city is the abundance of gold. A precious commodity throughout man's history, gold has been used as an overlay in works of art and as a standard of value, and has been the means of a great amount of both good and evil in society. It served the purposes of God in the tabernacle and temple, for much gold was in evidence there; it was also used by idolaters in the making of images. On earth, men have fought, suffered, and died for it. But in the New Jerusalem, gold will be so plentiful that it will be used for cobblestones and building blocks. And it will be like glass, possessing transparent qualities, so that the glorious light of the holy city will both shine through it and be reflected by it. Here is John's description:

> The city was pure gold, like clear glass. . . . and
> the street of the city was pure gold, like transparent
> glass (REV. 21:18,21).

Traditionally, gold has symbolized purity. In the wedding band, for example, the circle speaks of endlessness and the gold stands for purity. The golden street of the New Jerusalem, therefore, might well suggest the pure and holy walk of God's redeemed in their eternal home. And the brightness of the city, reflecting from the gold that abounds everywhere, will have its uncorrupted counterpart within the heart of every citizen of heaven. Yes, holiness and purity will pervade the eternal city.

Its Crystal River.

A river clear as crystal will flow through the New Jerusalem. The apostle John declared:

> *He showed me a pure river of water of life, clear as crystal, proceeding from the throne of God and of the Lamb* (REV. 22:1).

Just as in Eden there was a river to water the garden, so also in the New Jerusalem there will be a river of life. It will begin at the throne of God, the very uppermost part of the city, and it will course downward through the entire area.

Cities have always been dependent on a good water supply, providing for their inhabitants freshness, cleanness, and life. Even today the river continues to be an emblem of fruitfulness, vitality, and abundance, its waters being fed by melting snows from mountain ranges and refreshing springs, and constantly purified as they tumble downward to be used by people. In fact, our Savior very fittingly used the words "rivers of living water" (Jn. 7:38) to indicate the outflow of blessings from the life of the believer through the work of the Holy Spirit.

In the New Jerusalem, a river of crystal will flow forever, reminding us for all eternity that God has graciously and abundantly provided for our every spiritual need.

Remember, life in eternity will not be a nebulous existence in some nameless place. No indeed! We will lead rich and full lives in glorified bodies. We'll dwell on a renewed earth in a real city of gold, and our lives will be filled with significance and meaning as we give praise to our Redeemer and gladly do His bidding.

This crystal river flowing through our eternal home will be of sparkling beauty and of clarity beyond the purest water man has ever seen. Think of it! All who believe in Christ will walk the banks of this glorious crystal river. What a blessed joy will then be ours!

Its Tree Of Life.

A third item of special interest in the New Jerusalem will be the tree of life. When Adam and Eve sinned, the Lord God drove them from the Garden of Eden. One reason He did this was to prevent them from having further access to the tree of life. You see, they had rebelled, bringing the curse of death on themselves. The tree of life was therefore out of bounds for them. But in our eternal home we will once again be free to partake of the fruit of this tree, for Revelation 22 says:

In the middle of its street, and on either side of the river, was the tree of life (v. 2).

The term *tree of life* does not refer to one single tree, but to a species. Apparently there will be many such trees, for we are told that "on either side of the river, was the tree of life." While only one tree of life stood in Eden's garden, here in the New Jerusalem—man's eternal paradise—a multitude of these trees are seen lining the river and producing fruit continuously. Their leaves will be a special blessing to mankind, for John said that "the leaves of the tree were for the healing of the nations."

It's difficult to envision just how the trees, the crystal river, and the street of gold will be related. Some excellent Bible teachers feel that a river will flow through the middle of a broad street, and that alongside the river on each bank will be the trees. Others believe that a grove of trees is centered between the avenue of gold on one side and the river on the other. Regardless of which view you may choose, it's evident that those who conceive of heaven as a place where the redeemed will do nothing but sit on golden stairs playing harps are grossly mistaken. Life in heaven will be filled with beauty and variety. Christian friend, we've been concerned with what the Bible tells us about our eternal home. We have seen its beauty from without: its gleaming jasper walls, its jeweled foundations, and its gates of pearl. We have also seen its glory within as we have envisioned the street of gold, the crystal river, and the tree of life.

This glimpse of our eternal home should bring

two responses to the heart of the true believer in Christ. First, there should be a renewed determination to place top priority on the spiritual and eternal rather than on the physical and temporal. May we therefore, in anticipation of the glory and beauty of our eternal home, begin right now to "lay up . . . treasures in heaven" (Mt. 6:20) by putting the Lord first and by a constant willingness to serve Him.

Second, the thought of heaven should cheer us when we become discontented with life and discouraged about the future. No matter how badly things may be going or how difficult the struggles, the prospect of that wonderful abode awaiting us should be a source of encouragement and hope.

Remember, in heaven we will live forever in the presence of our loving Savior. Life will be rich and full, and we will know a purity, bliss, and love such as could never be experienced here.

The Home Of Blessedness

The pain, sorrow, and unhappiness in this world of ours are distressing to any sensitive individual. Starvation is rampant in some parts of the globe, mothers and their children have been left homeless by war, and young and old alike are destroying their lives inch by inch through alcohol and drug habits. Crime continues to be a problem. Selfishness and sin have turned our earthly home into a habitat of untold suffering and wickedness.

A time is coming, however, when all of this

will be changed. Our solar system will be purged by a great consuming fire, and it will be replaced by a new heaven and a new earth. Writing in Revelation 21 and 22, the apostle John recorded his vision of an immense city of shimmering beauty, descending slowly from heaven to become the capital city of our eternal home. It will be radiant with the light of God's glory shining through its jasper walls, its jeweled foundation, and its pearly gates. And this city, the New Jerusalem, will be the eternal abode of all who have placed their faith in Jesus Christ. All who have been saved will walk the street of gold in transformed, glorified bodies. We'll enjoy heaven's beautiful crystal river and have ready access to its tree of life. We'll be eternally delivered from every evil and burden that plagues our world today. And we'll finally have become what God intended us to be.

What a wonderful life we'll have in our eternal home! In that perfect society we'll realize our full spiritual potential as individuals. Having entered an eternal fellowship with God, we'll be engaged in an endless variety of meaningful activities. We'll join with the saints of all the ages in a spirit of communion, fellowship, and love, all centered on the Lord Jesus Christ.

In this concluding lesson on "Our Eternal Home," I'd like to consider with you some of the marvelous blessings that await us. We'll see that the imperfections of this life will be missing and that positive blessings will be there in abundance.

■ THE EFFECTS OF SIN REMOVED

So that we may more completely understand the blessings and glory of our life in heaven, John's record mentions a number of things that mar human existence on earth, and it assures us that they will not be present in our eternal home.

No Tears. Our days on earth are filled with tragedy, heartache, suffering, disappointment, and evil. As a result, tears are all too common in the experience of mankind. The lonely vigils at bedsides, the secret burdens buried deep in a mother's heart, and the memories of tragedy, rejection, and pain are all too close to us. But before eternity begins, God Himself will wipe away all tears from our eyes! The ministry will not be entrusted to angels. No lesser citizens of heaven will perform this task, for the Lord Himself will pour His healing balm into the wounds and hurts of our lives. The apostle John wrote:

> God will wipe away every tear from their eyes;
> there shall be no more death, nor sorrow, nor
> crying. There shall be no more pain, for the former
> things have passed away (REV. 21:4).

Let me be quick to point out that these words in no way imply that saints will shed tears in heaven concerning the sins and failures of their earthly lives. Not at all! The gracious, comforting work of God, not the remorse of the children, is the emphasis of this verse.

No Death. Not only will there be an absence of tears in heaven, but John also said, "There shall be no more death" (Rev. 21:4). This fearsome enemy continually casts its shadow on our lives here on earth. Eventually death enters every happy family circle. Sooner or later, every home experiences the feeling of emptiness—the dreadful vacuum caused by the passing of a loved one. No member of humanity, even the most strong, can escape the relentless passing of time and the realization that the earthly sojourn is brief. How happy we can be that in our eternal home we will experience no more anxiety, no more wondering when the end will come, no more long hours by hospital bedsides, and praise God, no more funerals!

No Sorrow Nor Crying. These words are closely related to the tears God wipes away, but the sorrow absent from our eternal home has reference to mourning or grief. Here on earth we have many occasions for sorrow—our own sins and shortcomings, personal misfortunes, disappointments in others, and distressing national conditions. When we reach the New Jerusalem, we shall never again mourn, but we'll be completely free from sin, experience no adversity or discouragement, and never have occasion to be concerned over calamitous national or world conditions. In James 4:9 sinners are warned to change their laughter into mourning, but in heaven the saints will exchange mourning for joy.

We also are reassured that there will be no more crying. This refers to loud, uncontrolled sobbing, the kind of weeping that results from the shock of deep, piercing hurt. Thank God, when we reach the eternal home, we will never again hear agonizing cries of sorrow or anguish. There will be no heartbreak in heaven.

No Pain. We are also given the comforting assurance that "there shall be no more pain" (Rev. 21:4). What a blessing to read these words from the Bible! A brief visit to a cancer ward, convalescent home, or hospital quickly gives us an unforgettable glimpse of the widespread suffering that curses our world. In heaven, however, we will never again experience hurt of any kind. These bodies of ours in their glorified state will be free from all disease. We'll never again know physical distress or suffering. And, we'll never grow old. A feeling of vigor and youthful energy will forever mark the resurrection body that will be ours.

No Night. Then too, we are told that night will never fall in heaven. The city had no need of the sun or of the moon to shine in it, for the glory of God illuminated it. The Lamb is its light. And the nations of those who are saved shall walk in its light, and the kings of the earth bring their glory and honor into it. Its gates shall not be shut at all by day (there shall be no night there) (Rev. 21:23-25).

In the present, we're dependent on the sun for light and heat. We have day and night, and the four seasons, because of the earth's rotation and our relationship to the sun. In heaven, however, there will be no need of sunlight, for the radiant glory of God will fill the city and spread throughout the entire earth.

No Defilement. Another element common to this life that will be missing in heaven will be defilement from evil. Revelation 21:27 tells us that "there shall by no means enter it anything that defiles, or causes an abomination or a lie." Today our society must deal with crime, violence, obscenity, and hatred. Pornographic literature, obscene theatrical productions, and blatant immorality pervade the culture. Parents are even afraid to let their children walk to the playground alone, for fear they will be harmed or molested. Drug addiction and its related evils and heartaches threaten our homes and families. Violent crimes such as rape, armed robbery, and murder plague our society.

The promise of no defilement in heaven, therefore, comes as good news. Within the gates of the New Jerusalem no sin can enter. No defiling substance nor personal acts of desecration can mar its eternal purity. And no spiritual or physical harm will ever come to any of God's children.

Think of it: No rebellion! No murder! No violence! No immorality! What a blessed place heaven will be!

No Curse. Another effect of sin that will be removed forever when we enter our eternal home is found in the promise that "there shall be no more curse" (Rev. 22:3). In our world, farmers must toil endlessly in their battle against weeds, poor soil, plant disease, and insects. A violent storm can wipe out a year's crops in a few minutes. But in heaven, nothing will impair productivity. All the effects of Adam's curse will be gone forever. Fields and orchards will flourish. Finally delivered from the consequences of Adam's fall, nature will smile on mankind. We'll experience an abundance that has been unknown since the fall of man.

In our eternal home, we will be free from tears, death, sorrow, crying, pain, darkness, and disappointment. How comforting and strengthening it is to reflect on the curse-free world that awaits us! The tears and sorrows of this life will only serve to make heaven all the sweeter.

■ MAN'S DESTINY FULFILLED

The evils that mar our life on earth will be gone in heaven, and we will fulfill perfectly the purpose for which God created us: to enjoy His presence, fellowship, and blessing. God has planned that we should be exalted above angels, for they are "sent forth to minister for those who will inherit salvation" (Heb. 1:14).

We Will Know Him Perfectly. Our present knowledge of God, while real and precious, remains incomplete. Sin has entered and distorted the picture, and we often fall short of the Lord's ideal for us. But in heaven we will know Him perfectly. We'll behold the glory of His presence, and faith will turn to sight.

I heard a loud voice from heaven saying, "Behold, the tabernacle of God is with men, and He will dwell with them, and they shall be His people. God Himself will be with them and be their God" (Rev. 21:3).

Yes, we will delight in the glory of the Lord God. And we will know Him personally, for the Bible says: They shall see His face, and His name shall be on their foreheads (Rev. 22:4).

Our hearts will throb with joy as we comprehend the fullness of the Lord's glory and majesty. Loving adoration and sincere praise will flow from our hearts as we gaze into the face of our Savior.

We Will Worship And Serve Him. In addition to the blessing of knowing and enjoying God, we will be kept busy in fruitful activity. There shall be no more curse, but the throne of God and of the Lamb shall be in it, and His servants shall serve Him (Rev. 22:3).

Sometimes heaven is incorrectly pictured as a place of never-ending boredom and sameness. Its inhabitants are portrayed as floating around on clouds, wearing long white robes, and playing harps all day. Or they are depicted as standing forever around the throne of God, mouthing His praises in unison for all eternity.

I'm glad that's not the accurate story. We'll worship God! It will be an important and rewarding part of our heavenly activity. The shortcomings and imperfections of our praise here will all be removed. Our minds won't wander during prayer as they do now, and we won't be thinking about business or other less important matters when our full attention should be directed toward God. No temple will be needed in the New Jerusalem (Rev. 21:22), for it would be an element of the imperfect, symbolic worship of this world.

The new world will also present opportunity for an endless variety of activities. The joys we derive from God's beautiful world of nature will still be ours, only on a far higher plane. The delight of fellowship with others will also exceed anything we have ever experienced on earth. In our heavenly home we will know one another perfectly, and each will be without fault. Our fellowship today is often marred by evasion and a covering of our deepest thoughts, but then a wonderful spirit-to-spirit communion of radiant personalities will exist. Remember, the verse said, "His servants shall serve Him." We'll be busy doing things He considers important, and we'll be infinitely happy as we do His will. Yes, in our eternal home we'll know a life of praise, satisfaction, and usefulness such as we have never experienced here on earth.

We Will Reign With Him. Finally, all believers in Christ will reign with the Lord Jesus for all eternity. The apostle John, after describing the light of God's glory that will surround us, revealed that we will share in His dominion over the earth. He declared:

> *There shall be no night there: They need no lamp nor light of the sun, for the Lord God gives them light. And they shall reign forever and ever (REV. 22:5).*

This completes our glorification. We will actually share in the authority of God over the transformed creation. Exalted far above the angels, transformed into the likeness of Jesus Christ, set free from all pain, sadness, sin, and death, we'll enjoy a life of never-ending happiness, satisfaction, and glory. We will have realized the purpose for which God made us, for with Jesus Christ we will exercise dominion over the earth.

You can make certain right now that heaven will be your eternal home by praying something like this:

"Lord Jesus, I want heaven to be my home. Therefore, believing that You died for me and arose from the grave, I accept You and the salvation You have provided. Forgive my sin. I'm trusting You and You alone for my salvation. Save me. I do believe. Amen."

If you prayed this sincerely, you can claim the promise of the Lord Jesus, "The one who comes to Me I will by no means cast out" (Jn. 6:37).